Josephine Baker

ENTERTAINER

Black Americans of Achievement

LEGACY EDITION

Muhammad Ali
Maya Angelou
Josephine Baker
Johnnie Cochran
Frederick Douglass
W.E.B. Du Bois
Marcus Garvey
Savion Glover
Alex Haley
Jimi Hendrix
Langston Hughes
Jesse Jackson
Scott Joplin
Coretta Scott King
Martin Luther King, Jr.
Malcolm X
Bob Marley
Thurgood Marshall
Jesse Owens
Rosa Parks
Colin Powell
Chris Rock
Sojourner Truth
Harriet Tubman
Nat Turner
Booker T. Washington
Oprah Winfrey

Black Americans of Achievement

LEGACY EDITION

Josephine Baker

ENTERTAINER

Alan Schroeder

With additional text written by
Heather Lehr Wagner

CHELSEA HOUSE
P U B L I S H E R S
An imprint of Infobase Publishing

Josephine Baker

Copyright © 2006 by Infobase Publishing

Chelsea House
An imprint of Infobase Publishing
132 West 31st Street
New York NY 10001

Library of Congress Cataloging-in-Publication Data

Schroeder, Alan.
  Josephine Baker / Alan Schroeder ; with additional text by Heather Lehr Wagner.
— Legacy ed.
     p. cm. — (Black Americans of achievement)
  Includes bibliographical references and index.
  ISBN 0-7910-9212-7 (hardcover)
 1. Baker, Josephine, 1906–1975—Juvenile literature 2. Dancers—France—Biography—
Juvenile literature. 3. African American entertainers—France—Biography—Juvenile litera-
ture. I. Wagner, Heather Lehr. II. Title. III. Series.
 GV1785.B3S37 2006
  792.8092—dc22   2006004583

Series and cover design by Keith Trego, Takeshi Takahashi

Printed in the United States of America

Bang FOF 10 9 8 7 6 5 4 3 2 1

This book is printed on acid-free paper.

Contents

Shuffle Along

On a rainy April day in 1921, 14-year-old Josephine Baker entered the Dunbar Theater in Philadelphia to audition for a new musical—a production that was likely bound for Broadway. Baker knew that she would soon lose her job with the Dixie Steppers when the vaudeville dancing troupe disbanded. The thin African-American girl needed money and wanted to dance. The opportunity to appear in a Broadway musical was a dream come true.

The musical for which Baker was auditioning was *Shuffle Along*, a bouncy, fast-paced production, with a toe-tapping score by Noble Sissle and Eubie Blake. The show, which had some of the most exuberant dancing ever seen on Broadway, would create a sensation when it opened in May 1921. *Shuffle Along*, in fact, would be the first truly successful African-American musical, running for more than 500 performances. Like *Show Boat* (1927) and *Oklahoma!* (1943), it is considered a landmark in the history of American musical theater.

But that afternoon in Philadelphia, the future of the show was still in doubt. The musical did not have enough financing; the costumes were left over from a previous show. Blake and Sissle could not afford to pay the chorus or the dancers until the show actually opened.

Baker was called forward to audition for Sissle, the show's lyricist, as well as for Flournoy Miller and Aubrey Lyles, the authors of the musical's book. Her energy and her stage presence impressed the group, but she was too thin and too small, and her skin was darker than that of the other girls they had hired for the chorus line. Also, she was obviously young, and New York State law forbade the hiring of chorus girls younger than 16. When they asked Baker her age, she lied and said she was 15. That was still too young, and so she was rejected.

Baker did not understand that her age had disqualified her. She had heard the men muttering about her skin color and size, and she was convinced that she had been rejected because her skin was too dark. She left the audition angry and dejected, her eyes full of tears as she walked out into the rain without even opening the umbrella she carried.

Shuffle Along opened at the Cort Theatre in New York on May 23, 1921. There were empty seats on the first night, but word quickly spread and soon the show was playing to packed houses. A midnight performance on Wednesdays was added so that other entertainers could see the show. Soon Blake and Sissle decided to form a road company, to send the musical production out on tour.

Meanwhile, Baker had not forgotten *Shuffle Along*. She had followed the show's triumphant first months in New York and was determined to become a part of that success. She decided to go to New York.

ANOTHER AUDITION

By now Baker was 15, still too young for the New York company. She had no close friends or relatives in New York. She slept on park benches for a few nights before finally managing to persuade someone at the theater to talk to her. She was granted an audition with the company's white manager, Al Mayer.

For the audition, Baker covered her face with light powder and, when asked her age, she replied that she was 17. Mayer felt she was too small and too skinny for the chorus line, but he offered her a job as a dresser for the road company.

Baker did not want to be a dresser. She wanted to perform. But she was reminded that, while traveling, chorus girls often became sick or left the company. If she learned all of the dances and songs, she might get a chance to fill in for an absent chorus girl.

Baker went on the road, spending her time caring for the costumes and helping the performers put them on and take them off each night. In her memoir *Josephine*, Baker noted her frustration: "The dancers looked discouragingly healthy, and it was all I could do to keep myself from wishing for a magic potion that would strike one of them down."

Then, one night, she got her chance. Just before show time, a member of the chorus became sick. It turned out she was pregnant. As the manager fumed and worried, Baker casually mentioned to him that she knew all the songs and dances. Within moments, she was dressed and out on the stage.

Then the magic took over—the magic that had always swept over Baker when she stepped onto a stage. She began to dance, moving her arms and legs wildly, responding to a rhythm that only she could hear. She did not blend in with the rest of the chorus line—she tripped while they kicked, she crossed her eyes while they moved gracefully. The audience, though, loved her performance—they laughed and cheered every time she appeared on stage. The other performers were furious, accusing Baker of stealing scenes.

Positive reviews appeared, reviews that specifically mentioned Baker's performance. Ticket-buyers asked if the comic

In a few short years, Josephine Baker would go from a gangly 14-year-old who dreamed of being in a Broadway-bound show to a star in New York and Paris—an exotic star who would harness an ostrich to pull a racing sulky, above.

chorus girl who crossed her eyes was appearing. Baker was becoming as famous as the show.

TOURING AMERICA

Soon the positive reviews came to the attention of *Shuffle Along*'s creators, Sissle and Blake. When the touring company traveled to Brooklyn, Sissle and Blake were in the audience. Sissle quickly recognized the young girl who had auditioned in Philadelphia, and the two men went backstage to speak with her.

Baker was afraid that she was going to be fired, and she quickly lied, telling them that she was now 16. They reassured her that age was not an issue for the touring company. In fact, rather than firing her, they wanted to offer her a position with the main company when the touring company ended its run that summer.

By the summer, however, *Shuffle Along* had closed on Broadway, and the main company went out on tour. Baker joined the main company in Boston in August 1922. The show played there for four months to enthusiastic audiences and then traveled on to Chicago, receiving the same acclaim during a 15-week run.

Blake and Sissle took Baker under their wing, teaching her discipline as well as the more subtle skills of performing onstage. Sissle tried to choreograph routines with her, but the second Baker was onstage, she had forgotten all they had discussed and began to improvise a series of wild, funny moves and dance steps. Because what she improvised was generally far better than what they had planned, Sissle did not object.

But Baker was learning—learning discipline, and learning to plan a routine so it led from move to move to form a pattern that could enthrall audiences. Thanks to Sissle, she began

IN HER OWN WORDS...

In her memoir *Josephine,* Baker noted that, after her first appearance in *Shuffle Along,* the positive reviews for her performance made the other members of the chorus line jealous:

> At the box office, people began asking, "Is this the show with the little cross-eyed girl?" I had become the star of the chorus, much to the disgust of my fellow dancers. "Monkey," they called me, and did what they could to make my life backstage miserable. I finally took to dressing in the bathroom. At least no one bothered me there! One of the dancers even tripped me up one night as we were making our entrance, but I managed to do such a comical nose dive that I received more applause than ever. They didn't try *that* again!

Eubie Blake plays the piano as his performing partner, Noble Sissle,
jots down notes. Blake and Sissle's musical *Shuffle Along* became
one of the first truly successful African-American musicals. After seeing Josephine Baker in a touring production of the show, the two men
began to act as her mentors.

to think of herself as an artist, rather than simply a comedienne. She began to imagine herself on stage without the rolling eyes and crazy gestures, to imagine herself as a stage presence, rather than a clown.

Baker remained with *Shuffle Along* as it toured the United States, performing in the show for almost two years until it finally closed in January 1924. The teenager from St. Louis had made herself an integral part of one of the most exciting and successful African-American musicals in history and had become a protégé of two great theatrical talents. She had learned skills that would shape her career for the rest of her life. She had received extraordinary reviews and had performed in cities all over the country.

But this was only the beginning of Baker's story. She would join Sissle and Blake's next production, earning the exceptional sum of $125 a week and the title of "the highest-paid chorus girl in the world." She would travel to France and become the toast of Paris and one of the most famous and wealthy women in that glittering capital. When Nazi troops seized French territory, Baker would become a spy, supplying the French Resistance with valuable information. She would also challenge discrimination in America.

But the beginning of her story is not found in a theater. It begins instead in a slum in St. Louis, Missouri.

2

Childhood in Boxcar Town

The woman who would become a vibrant symbol of the beauty and power of African-American culture was born into poverty to a washerwoman and a musician who quickly abandoned his family. The woman who would become Josephine Baker was born on June 3, 1906, in St. Louis, Missouri, and given the name Freda Josephine McDonald. Her mother soon gave her the nickname "Tumpie," an accidental variation on Humpty Dumpty, because she thought her stout baby resembled a roly-poly egg. ("Mama," Baker admitted years later, "hadn't heard the poem quite right.")

Josephine's mother, Carrie McDonald, arrived in St. Louis in 1904 to seek a better life for herself. She was able to find work quickly, taking in laundry and keeping house for well-to-do white families. A hard worker, Carrie also had dreams of becoming an entertainer, and it was during a local production of a play that she met Eddie Carson, who would become Josephine's father.

Eddie Carson was a fun-loving drummer who performed in the smoky barrelhouses and gambling halls that made up the notorious section of town called Chestnut Valley. Like most musicians, Eddie played because he loved music. In the early 1900s, there was no better place for a drummer to find work than in St. Louis. Musically, it was one of the most important cities in the nation, attracting many gifted ragtime composers. It was there, on the banks of the Mississippi River, that Scott Joplin wrote some of his earliest piano music.

Because Eddie spent more and more time away from home, Carrie began to take Josephine to the crowded gambling halls and dimly lighted honky-tonks to hear Eddie and his friends play. These jazzmen were performing the most exciting music in the country, and many of Josephine's earliest memories were of the sounds of St. Louis.

Not long after Josephine's birth, Carrie had another baby, a boy named Richard. But Eddie was increasingly absent from home. He was not ready for the demands of fatherhood, demands that might take him away from the music he loved. In time, he packed his belongings and moved out.

The family had never had much money, and Eddie's departure made getting by even more difficult for Carrie and her children. With two small children to feed, Carrie had limited options. She eventually chose marriage as a way to help improve her family's financial situation, marrying a factory worker named Arthur Martin, a moody fellow who felt that life had never given him a fair shake. Unfortunately, Arthur's quick temper made it difficult for him to hold down a job for any length of time, and Carrie was forced to take in laundry to pay the bills. Life, it often seemed, was nothing but one long struggle to pay the rent (or figure out a way not to pay it). The family was always moving, always trying to stay one step ahead of the landlord.

In time, Carrie had two more daughters, Margaret and Willie Mae. To make things easier for the family, Josephine was frequently sent to live with Grandma McDonald, a warm, loving woman who liked to bake cookies and read bedtime stories to her granddaughter. These stories, fairy tales mostly, filled Josephine's head with visions of princes, castles, white horses and beautiful women. They helped her escape, at least for a little while, the hardships of home.

One Sunday, while returning from church, Josephine stepped on a rusty nail, which pierced her foot. By the time she got home, her leg was swollen from blood poisoning. Carrie rushed her to the doctor, who recommended that the leg be cut off. Josephine took one look at the amputation saw and became hysterical.

To calm her down, the doctor slowly drained the wound. Josephine nearly fainted when she saw that her blood had turned black. Fortunately, her leg did not need to be amputated, although nearly a month passed before she could walk normally. The doctor's bill became yet another burden for the family.

DREAMS OF FREEDOM

Each morning, Arthur walked to one of the factories in St. Louis and waited at the gate to see if there was any work that day. Landing a job was largely a matter of being in the right place at the right time, and Arthur rarely was. While Carrie prepared dinner, he would bitterly complain about society, about how difficult it was for an African American to get ahead in St. Louis.

Many evenings, after their meal, Arthur would tell Josephine and the other children about a dream he had. He believed that the day would come when all people would be free—free of prejudice, free of hate—and on that glorious day, people of all races would live together in harmony. Trust would be their common bond. It was a hope that Arthur cherished. Like Carrie's deep belief in God, Arthur's dream somehow made the burden of life seem a little lighter.

Besides Arthur's dreams and Grandma McDonald's fairy tales, there was always music to comfort Josephine. St. Louis was alive with it. Music could be heard in the cafés and wine rooms in the afternoons, and it heated up the honky-tonks every night. Long after the sun had gone down, Josephine would lie in bed and listen to the lively sounds of ragtime, as well as a sadder, more haunting kind of music: the blues.

Josephine's parents had performed together in the city's vaudeville houses, so it was only natural that Josephine took an interest in performing, too. She began to dance for a practical reason, too: to keep herself warm during the cold Missouri winters. When spring came, however, she continued to dance because it made her happy and, like the fairy tales, dancing helped her forget the family's troubles.

Every now and then, when she could afford it, Josephine went to the Booker T. Washington Theater, a black vaudeville house at 23rd and Market. Famous black entertainers like Ma Rainey and Bessie Smith performed there frequently, and in the darkness of that small theater, Josephine could lose herself in a

IN HER OWN WORDS...

Music and dance formed a part of Josephine Baker's world from the time she was a young girl in St. Louis. In her memoir *Josephine*, she shared her memory of this early influence:

I spent most of my time wandering around the colored quarter. Unlike Aunt Elvara, who detested our neighborhood, I thought it was terribly exciting. Especially on Saturdays. Everyone seemed to own an accordion, a banjo or harmonica. Those without enough money for real instruments made banjos from cheese boxes. We played music that to us was beautiful on everything from clothesline strung across barrel halves to paper-covered combs. As soon as the music began, I would move my arms and legs in all directions in time to the rhythm or mark the beat with my friends on the treasure we pulled from the trash: tin cans, battered saucepans, abandoned wooden and metal containers. What a wonderful time we had!

world of bright lights, pretty costumes, and wonderful music. She especially liked to watch the chorus girls as they sashayed their way across the stage, legs kicking, feathers flying.

To amuse themselves, the neighborhood children began to stage their own vaudeville shows, copying whatever was playing that week at the Washington Theater. Admission to the children's show cost a penny, and Josephine usually made up half of the two-girl chorus line. During these simple productions, Josephine began to think that someday she might like to be a dancer.

As Josephine grew older, however, she discovered she had less and less time to dream. As the eldest child, she had to begin pulling her own weight. Schooling was all right, Carrie felt, but it was more important for a young black girl to learn household chores, which would enable her to earn a living. And so Josephine was sent to live with a Mrs. Keiser, who gave the child room and board in exchange for household work.

As it turned out, the arrangement was less than fair. Keiser was a cruel woman who worked Josephine constantly, beating her with a stick until blisters appeared on her back. The evening meals were never plentiful, and Josephine's bed was nothing more than a wooden box in the cellar, which she had to share with a crippled dog named Three Legs.

This unhappy arrangement ended when Josephine accidentally cracked some dinner plates. Keiser, in a fit of anger, seized Josephine's arm and plunged it into a pot of boiling water. The pain was so great that Josephine fainted. When she awoke, she was in a hospital.

As soon as she was well, Josephine needed to look for another job. In the winter, she earned a few coins by going from house to house and shoveling snow; in the summer, she rang doorbells and offered to baby-sit or scrub floors. She gave what little money she made to Carrie, usually keeping a nickel for herself. Five nickels, after all, was enough to get into the Booker T. Washington Theater.

Blues singer Bessie Smith (shown here) used to perform at the Booker T. Washington Theater, a black vaudeville house in St. Louis. As a youngster, Josephine Baker would save up her nickels so she could attend shows at the Booker T.

BOXCAR TOWN RIOT

By this time, Josephine's family was living in a one-room shack in Boxcar Town, an area in East St. Louis, Illinois, across the Mississippi River from St. Louis. The neighborhood was dirty and depressing. True to its name, many of the "houses" were nothing more than abandoned boxcars.

Arthur did his best to make the shack livable, hanging scraps of newspaper on the wall for wallpaper. Realizing how much it meant to Josephine, Carrie allowed her to raise two puppies, which she fed old pieces of bread dipped in Sunday's milk. But these small gestures barely helped to make life in Boxcar Town more agreeable.

Rats, the family discovered, were a constant menace, and flattened tin cans were hammered over the holes in the floor to keep them out. This tactic rarely worked: The rats gnawed through the metal. Terrified, Josephine would watch as her brother, Richard, sat up in bed and picked off the rats with a slingshot.

Sometimes, there was not enough money to buy food, and Josephine spent many afternoons searching through the trash for a fish head or a spoiled potato to put in her mother's soup. At times, it seemed as if life could not get any harder.

One evening in July 1917, Josephine was asleep in bed when she suddenly felt her patchwork quilt being yanked back. Before she could understand what was happening, Carrie had pulled her to her feet, begging her to get dressed as quickly as she could. It was a frightening moment, full of confusion and panic. As Arthur lit a lantern, Josephine watched her mother tear through the bureau drawers, frantically grabbing what little money the family had.

Carrie had good reason to be afraid. A half-hour earlier, East St. Louis had exploded in a racial riot. Warnings sped through the back alleys, but for many it was too late. By the time Carrie managed to push her family outdoors, the sky was already red with flames, and the night air was filled with screams as African Americans were hunted down and clubbed in the streets. Fences were trampled, windows were shattered, and boxcars exploded in violent flames.

Clutching her two puppies to her chest, Josephine felt herself pushed to the ground. Carrie covered her children as best she could, while dozens of terrified families ran through the streets, dragging their few possessions behind them in broken-down baby carriages. A few feet from where Carrie was crouching, an African-American man was knocked to the ground; a

The East St. Louis Riot of 1917

In 1916 and 1917, 10,000 to 12,000 African Americans migrated from the South to East St. Louis, drawn by the promise of jobs in the wartime industries based there. Until that time, the population of East St. Louis had largely been white, and the arrival of so many African Americans to claim jobs in the city's industrial plants sparked a rise in racial tensions. Many blacks landed jobs at the local factories because they were not paid as much as white workers. The lower-class whites bitterly resented this situation. Labor agitators intensified the problem by spreading lurid rumors of atrocious crimes committed by people of color. Signs in the windows of gun shops urged passers-by to buy guns to protect themselves.

On July 1, 1917, these tensions exploded when a rumor that a black man had killed a white man began to spread through the streets. The next day, violence erupted, targeting African-American communities like the Boxcar Town area where Baker lived. There were shootings, beatings, and arson. The violence and rioting continued for nearly a week. When it finally ended, 9 whites and 39 African Americans had been killed, according to official reports, although authorities believe many more blacks were killed. Some 6,000 African Americans left the city, fearing for their lives.

On July 28, the National Association for the Advancement of Colored People (NAACP) marched down Fifth Avenue in New York City, to protest the riot and other acts of violence against black Americans. The United States had only recently entered World War I, and German propaganda exploited the race riot in an effort to arouse antiwar sentiment within America's black community. East St. Louis became so closely identified with racial violence and rioting that the city never fully recovered. The population leveled off at 75,000 in 1920, and experienced little demographic growth in the years that followed.

Members of the National Association for the Advancement of Colored People (NAACP) marched down New York City's Fifth Avenue in late July 1917. The march was to protest the East St. Louis riot and other killings of African Americans in the United States.

moment later, a white man began to beat him savagely with a club. It was a horrifying and bloody scene, one that Josephine would never forget. In later years, she always referred to the East St. Louis riot as the worst memory of her childhood.

After several hours, the melee finally came to an end. The flames in the boxcars died, having nothing left to feed upon. Emergency first-aid and shelter stations were set up, and with the arrival of dawn, the now-homeless black community returned to salvage what it could from the smoking debris. In all, 39 black people and 9 white people had been killed. Property damage exceeded a half-million dollars.

The riot, understandably, was a turning point in Josephine's life. As she walked past the long lines of people waiting for Red Cross handouts, she realized, perhaps for the first time, that she would have to be strong, very strong, to survive in a white man's world. According to Josephine, she made a vow that day that when she became an adult, she would try to make it easier for whites and blacks to get along. At that moment, however, Arthur's dream of universal brotherhood must have seemed nearly impossible.

3

On the Road

In addition to the panic and fear of that bloody night, the East St. Louis riot of 1917 left the African-American community homeless. Many had lost all of their possessions to the fires and violence, and those who did escape with their lives faced severe financial hardship. Josephine's mother, Carrie, once more shouldered the burden of making sure that her family survived. Arthur was still unemployed, so Carrie began to take in more laundry than ever. As the oldest child, Josephine was also expected to take on additional responsibilities to help the family earn enough money for food and shelter. Josephine was ordered to help her mother with the laundry work, and she spent long hours scrubbing trousers and petticoats in the sink. The work was dull, dreary, and hard, and Josephine hated every minute of it. She saw washing as a dead-end life and firmly vowed not to repeat her mother's fate.

Desperate to escape the tedium of laundry work, Josephine became a waitress at the Old Chauffeur's Club on Pine Street. The work was not easy, but it was a lot more enjoyable than scrubbing, and besides, the Old Chauffeur's Club was next to Pythian Hall, where Eddie Carson's band was playing. Eddie enjoyed the hours he spent with his daughter, and Josephine loved listening to the band.

By now, 13-year-old Josephine was eager to escape the confines of her family life. She envied her father's freedom and his ability to travel and play wherever he wanted. And so it is perhaps not surprising that she seized the first opportunity for freedom that presented itself to her. It came in the person of a foundry worker named Willie Wells, whom Josephine probably met at a neighborhood dance. The naive young girl knew little of life or men. Her focus was on escaping the misery at home. So she decided to marry Willie Wells.

The marriage did not last long, ending one night when the newlyweds got into a violent fight. Josephine broke a bottle to defend herself, and Willie stormed out of the house, never to reappear. A confused and unhappy Josephine returned to her job as a waitress at the Old Chauffeur's Club. Now her focus was shifting: She no longer simply wanted to escape her life at home, she wanted to get out of St. Louis altogether.

Josephine soon found a way out. In late 1919, she met a ragtag trio of performers called the Jones Family Band. Old Man Jones played a brass horn, his wife played the trumpet, and their pretty daughter, Doll, was a fiddler. During her breaks at the Old Chauffeur's Club, Josephine entertained the customers by singing songs and doing a few easy dance steps. Old Man Jones liked what he saw and, on the spur of the moment, he invited her to join their trio. Josephine needed no time to think about the idea. On the spot, she quit her job and joined the Jones Family Band.

The Jones family did not pay Josephine for her work, although they did teach her to play the trombone. Performing in cafés and restaurants and barbershops was exhausting, even embarrassing, and sometimes Josephine wondered if she had made the right decision.

The hard work, however, eventually paid off. The Jones Family Band was invited to play for a week at the Booker T. Washington Theater. Opening night was memorable. Josephine's costume was much too big for her, but instead of letting the long dress interfere with her dancing, she cleverly, and humorously, made it the visual focus of the act. Even at this early stage of her career, Josephine seemed to understand the fundamentals of theatrical comedy. Rolling her eyes outrageously, she was a natural comedienne, and the audience rewarded her nightly with gales of laughter.

The Dixie Steppers were the stars of the show, and the Steppers and the Jones Family Band were asked to stay on for a second week. They did, and at the end of the engagement, another invitation came, this one even more unexpected: The Steppers asked the Jones Family Band to join them on their tour of the South. Old Man Jones agreed to go, then asked Josephine if she would be coming. After all, he explained, she was part of the Family now.

IN HER OWN WORDS...

When the Jones Family Band took its act on the road, Josephine Baker went along, believing she could never be a star if she stayed in St. Louis. In her memoir *Josephine*, she recalled the moment when she left her home behind:

> We left by the night train. I had never seen curtains as pretty as those in the Pullman car windows. From my seat at Mrs. Russell's side, her cigar smoke pricking my nose, I peered nervously out the window, looking for Mama's angry face, Grandma's reproachful eyes, or the stern gaze of Daddy or Aunt Jo. No, Daddy Arthur would already be in bed, so full of beer that nothing could wake him. I was safely on my way. Closing my eyes, I dreamed of sunlit cities, magnificent theaters and me in the limelight.

Sensing how important this opportunity was, Josephine quickly agreed. At long last, she had her chance—her chance to escape St. Louis, to get away from the dirty dishes at the Old Chauffeur's Club and the piles of laundry in Carrie's apartment. She immediately hurried home, told her mother what had happened, threw her things into an old suitcase, and boarded the midnight train for Tennessee.

AN ENTERTAINER'S EDUCATION

Life on the road, Josephine discovered, was entirely different from anything she had ever experienced. It was exhilarating, it was exhausting, and it was also a little frightening. After the riot of 1917, Josephine had become increasingly aware of discrimination and the wide gap that divided white Americans from people of color. Unfortunately, the discrimination intensified as she traveled farther south.

Dancing off the train, swinging their baggage and cracking vaudeville jokes, the Dixie Steppers and the Jones Family Band were frequently met with cold, unfriendly stares. Porters refused to help them with their heavy trunks, and it was nearly impossible to find a room in a decent boardinghouse. Lunch counters, public restrooms, streetcars, and water fountains were all strictly segregated. Josephine grew to hate the familiar cardboard signs that read "For Whites Only."

In the years immediately after World War I, African-American entertainment had not yet come into its own. Bessie Smith, Ida Cox, and Ma Rainey all had loyal followings, but these singers were the exceptions. In 1920, "Negro vaudeville" (as it was called) was a rough-and-tumble affair. Most of the theaters Josephine encountered were cold, seedy firetraps, with dripping pipes, makeshift chairs, and scurrying cockroaches. Candles provided the only light, and the small pickup orchestra was usually out of tune. Now that she could see it for what it was, the world of vaudeville was disappointing, but in Josephine's opinion, it was still a lot better than scrubbing dirty clothes.

Her work involved far more than simply performing. Josephine was expected to help the Steppers with their props, or sew costumes, or pack the trunks. Every day was different on the vaudeville circuit, and Josephine learned as much as she could as quickly as she could. She was like a sponge, picking up all the tricks of the trade.

One of the most important tricks was learning how to get laughs. In her opening scene with the Jones Family Band, Josephine played a winged Cupid suspended from the rafters. During one performance, though, her pasteboard wings got caught on the curtain. The harder she struggled to release herself, the harder the audience laughed. After a stagehand carefully lowered her to safety, the manager came running up. Josephine, in tears, was certain she was going to be fired. Instead, the manager raved about her comic performance and insisted she do it the same way every night. Cupid's clumsy appearance became the highlight of the show.

By the time the troupe arrived in New Orleans, Josephine considered herself an experienced performer. Her only worry was her body. A thin child, with bean-pole legs and an average face, she wondered if she would ever be pretty enough to be a chorus girl. She toyed with the idea of appearing in whiteface, but Clara Smith, the star of the show, assured her that talent, not skin color, was what mattered in show business. To fatten Josephine up, however, Clara began to feed her thick slices of sweet potato pie before each matinee.

Near the end of the New Orleans engagement, the members of the Jones Family Band decided they had had enough of the vaudeville circuit. When Old Man Jones announced that his family was quitting the business, Josephine was shocked.

A second bombshell dropped when the Dixie Steppers told Josephine that without the Jones Family Band they had no place for her in their act. For the Steppers, Josephine was too light-skinned. She did not fit in with the rest of the chorus girls.

Josephine Baker mugs for the camera in a photograph taken in Paris in the mid-1920s. During her stint in vaudeville with the Jones Family Band and the Dixie Steppers, Baker learned how to get laughs. "I became the show's 'funny girl,'" she remembered.

Josephine panicked. She desperately wanted to stay in vaudeville. So, at the end of the New Orleans engagement, she did a daring thing. As the Steppers prepared to move on to another town, she slipped into one of their unlocked shipping crates, which was hoisted onto the train with the rest of the baggage. Three hours later, she emerged, half-frozen, the tips of her fingers blue from the cold.

The Dixie Steppers were highly annoyed, but they also admired Josephine's determination. They decided to hire her at nine dollars a week, even though they were still unsure how to fit her into the act. She would be an "odds-and-ends girl," doing whatever needed to be done at the moment.

FUNNY GIRL

Having forced her way into the Dixie Steppers' troupe, Josephine was determined to work twice as hard, repairing costumes, polishing shoes, painting scenery, sewing buttons, passing out handbills on street corners. She was eager to do anything, anything at all, to get on the stage and make people laugh and applaud. She never fit in with the rest of the chorus, but the Steppers quickly realized that maybe that was not such a bad thing. Josephine had personality—people laughed when she came onstage. In vaudeville, where so much depended on visual humor, that was a rare gift. "I became the show's 'funny girl,'" Josephine remembered.

After touring the Southern states, the Steppers turned north, eventually pulling into Philadelphia. There, Josephine met an easygoing young man named William Howard Baker. Willie, as she called him, was a Pullman porter, and the two hit it off immediately. Willie was impressed with her exciting life as an entertainer; she, in turn, admired his honest and gentle nature. As a vaudevillian, Josephine led a life of constant change, and at the age of 14, she saw Willie as a source of stability. He could be the family she missed so much. As the weeks slipped by, their friendship blossomed into romance.

During the Philadelphia engagement, an unsettling event occurred. The manager announced that the show was disbanding. Within days, each person in the cast had gone his or her separate way, and Josephine's weekly salary was a thing of the past. Marriage seemed like a safe and sensible move so, a few months later, in September 1921, Josephine married Willie Baker. The marriage turned out to be a disappointment, but it did give Josephine one important thing—the name Baker, which she would use for the rest of her career.

After the collapse of the show in early 1921, Josephine knew she had to find work quickly. When she heard that tryouts were being held for *Shuffle Along*, a new, Broadway-bound musical, she threw on her coat and hurried to the Dunbar Theater for an audition.

Josephine's eventual appearance in the chorus of *Shuffle Along* was one of the most important events of her life. Not only was the work steady, but it also gave her an opportunity to refine her comedic talents, talents that would soon make her one of the brightest stars in vaudeville.

4

La Revue Nègre

Josephine Baker discovered that being part of an established hit like *Shuffle Along* made life on the road a very different experience. She was pleased to find that the theaters were cleaner, the orchestras were more professional, and the audience even included some white people, who had heard about the show when it was in New York and wanted to see it for themselves. Many aspects of the tour remained the same, however: the cold hotel rooms, the loneliness, the hurried meals, the long hours spent getting from one city to another.

The racial discrimination that Baker had so vividly experienced in the South reared its ugly head again. This time it came not only from whites but also from other members of the cast. Nearly all of the chorus girls in *Shuffle Along* were light-skinned, and they were proud of it. They looked down on Baker because her skin was darker than theirs. They called her "the monkey" and played cruel tricks on her, stealing her hairbrushes and gluing her shoes to the floor. It did not take long for Baker to realize that if she was ever going to get ahead, she would have to rely upon herself. No one was going to make it easy for her.

Shuffle Along ended its run in early 1924. When the time came later that year to select the cast for Sissle and Blake's newest musical, Baker was hired immediately. The show was called *The Chocolate Dandies*, and for the first time she was given a chance to step out of the chorus and appear in several of the knockabout comedy sketches. *The Chocolate Dandies* was not a great success, but Baker received excellent reviews. When the show closed, she was offered a job at the Plantation Club at 50th and Broadway.

The Plantation Club was an elite nightclub for wealthy New Yorkers. Mobsters and millionaires flocked to see the club's popular revue. Baker considered it the most elegant place she had ever seen. The waiters spoke French, the tablecloths were freshly starched, and Ethel Waters, the blues singer, was the star of the show.

As always, Baker was determined to learn from the more experienced performers she encountered, eager to perfect her skills. Each evening, from her place in the chorus line, Baker studied Waters's mannerisms, her rich aching voice, and her dramatic choice of songs: "St. Louis Blues," "Georgia Blues," "My Man." Baker herself had a pleasing but rather thin voice; in the afternoons, while the waiters set the tables and the floor was being swept, she practiced her singing, trying to copy Waters's deep, robust sound.

The practice paid off. One evening, the star came down with laryngitis, and Baker was asked to sing one of Waters's most popular songs, "Dinah." She was extremely nervous as she walked to the microphone, but the audience did not seem to notice. At the end of the song, Baker received a tremendous round of applause.

An experienced performer like Waters was not going to be upstaged by a chorus girl. The very next evening, Waters was

Singer and actress Ethel Waters is shown above in a photograph from 1940. Fifteen years earlier, Waters had been the headliner at the Planta-tion Club in New York City, and chorus girl Josephine Baker studied her performances. When Waters had laryngitis one night, Baker sang one of Waters's most popular songs, "Dinah," to much acclaim.

back onstage and Baker was back in the chorus. And that is where she remained. After a few months, Baker realized that the Plantation Club already had a star—it did not need two. Her part in this production would never be any larger.

At this point, as she was beginning to look around for a new opportunity, Baker's career took a surprising turn. One evening, a smartly dressed white woman came to Baker's dressing room and, extending a manicured hand, she introduced herself as Caroline Dudley. In businesslike fashion, she explained that she and a partner, André Daven, were producing a show of black vaudeville in Paris. She had come to the United States to find dancers and for weeks had been visiting every nightclub and speakeasy in Harlem. That evening, she caught Baker's performance and was greatly impressed by her comic talents. Then, very casually, Dudley asked Baker if she would like to come with her to Paris.

Baker was speechless. As soon as she could collect her wits, though, she realized that the offer was extremely risky. Dudley's show might fail, and Baker did not relish the idea of being stranded in a foreign country with no money and no way to get home.

There was a self-assurance about Dudley, however, that eased these fears. Timing, she told Baker, was everything, and in Paris the time was right for black vaudeville. She was certain *La Revue Nègre* would be a success.

Two factors ultimately decided Baker's future. The first, of course, was show business. Any chorus girl would have given her eyeteeth to have been in Baker's shoes. The second factor, and one that was equally important, was discrimination. Years later, Baker captured her feelings on paper, and in doing so, she expressed the bitterness and the sadness that many African Americans were feeling at the time:

France ... I had dreamed of going there ever since Albert, one of the waiters at the Plantation, had shown me a photograph of the Eiffel Tower. It looked very different from the Statue of Liberty, but what did that matter? What was the good of having the statue without the liberty, the freedom to go where one chose if one was held back by one's color? No, I preferred the Eiffel Tower, which made no promises. I had sworn to myself that I would see it one day. And suddenly here was my chance.

SAILING TO FRANCE

On September 15, 1925, Baker sailed for Paris aboard the RMS *Berengaria*, one of 25 dancers and musicians whom Dudley had hired for the new show. As the ship pulled away from New York Harbor, Dudley chatted about Paris, describing in great detail the elegant theaters, the charming cafés, and the many delights of the Champs-Élysées.

Two members of the cast had been to Paris before, and Baker quickly befriended one of them, Sidney Bechet. A gifted clarinetist, Bechet assured her that everything was different in

The Harlem Renaissance

The cultural revolution that took place between the two world wars in the section of New York City known as Harlem marked a rise in the impact of black Americans on the arts. The Harlem Renaissance influenced dance, music, literature, and even politics.

Among the many black Americans who shaped this renaissance were musicians Duke Ellington and Cab Calloway, singer Bessie Smith, and writers Langston Hughes and Zora Neale Hurston. Their work represented a return to African roots, as these artists used traditional African rhythms and movements, the cadences of spirituals, and the pictures of ordinary life to create a fusion of new and old. Through contributions to the arts, these talented men and women were able to support the movement toward civil rights and equality.

Racism and discrimination, however, forced many African-American artists abroad. Many, like Baker, moved to Paris. Actor and opera singer Paul Robeson was another artist who found fame only when he left the United States and began to perform in Europe.

France, especially when it came to racial discrimination. Baker, he said, would be treated the same as any white person.

The second night out, a gala was held for the first-class passengers. Dudley, to cut down on expenses, had arranged for the troupe to perform. Unfortunately, the event proved to be Baker's first professional disaster.

Dudley suggested that she dance the Charleston, but Baker refused. She wanted to be taken seriously. Remembering her success with "Dinah" at the Plantation Club, she decided to sing "Brown Eyes," a sentimental blues number. The acoustics in the large room, however, were poor, and Baker could hardly hear herself. She lost the beat a few bars into the song. Her voice cracked; she hit wrong notes. She barely managed to finish the number.

Dudley later explained to the teenager that she was too young to sing torch songs. More important, they were not her style. If Baker wanted to succeed in show business, Dudley told her, she would have to develop a keen sense of her strengths and weaknesses. She was a fine dancer, and she could make people laugh. Dudley encouraged her to cultivate these talents. With luck, they would make her famous.

The rest of the seven-day voyage was spent in rehearsals. Dudley worked her dancers hard, nervously watching them as they shuffled and strutted their way across the ballroom floor. La Revue Nègre was the first show she had ever produced, and she wondered how the Parisians would respond to the brash, enthusiastic quality of the performance.

The company arrived in Paris on the morning of September 22. It was raining lightly, and the dancers were quickly driven to the Théâtre des Champs-Élysées, a large concrete building on the avenue Montaigne. Laughing, shouting, and swinging their baggage, the troupe tap-danced across the sidewalk and into the lobby of the elegant theater. The show, they were told, was to open in 10 days.

As the first rehearsal got under way, a young French artist entered the theater and began an assignment that would change Baker's career forever. The artist, Paul Colin, sat in the back row of the theater, making one quick sketch after another. It was his job to create the poster for *La Revue Nègre*. Timing was crucial: The artwork had to be at the printer the following day. Colin wanted the poster to be special, one that would capture the knee-slapping enthusiasm of the dancers. As he worked, his eye caught Baker stepping into the spotlight. Kicking out her coffee-colored legs, she began to dance a snappy Charleston. This was exactly the inspiration Colin needed. To a young Frenchman, Baker was the very essence of Harlem: exotic and colorful, vibrant and dynamic.

The next day, the completed poster—featuring Baker dancing—was rushed to the printer. It would soon appear on billboards and kiosks throughout Paris, creating tremendous excitement. The posters became so popular, in fact, that many were stolen before the show even opened.

By the end of the week, Caroline Dudley was putting the finishing touches on her revue. Every afternoon, Paul Colin returned to his seat at the back of the theater to watch Baker perform her frantic Charleston. At night, he showed her the beauty of Paris by dark: the Champs-Élysées, the Arc de Triomphe, the Eiffel Tower, the intimate cafés, and rollicking cabarets. In no time, Baker had fallen in love with the City of Light.

What impressed her most about Paris was the atmosphere of total freedom. When Baker went to a restaurant or the cinema, she was treated just like everyone else. She did not need to step off the sidewalk or cross the street when a white person approached, as she was expected to do in the United States. She could go anywhere she wanted, do anything she liked. It was a wonderful feeling to an African American.

BLACK VENUS

By October 2, the cast and crew were ready, the posters had created tremendous buzz, and all of Paris seemed eager to see this new entertainment. The show opened to a packed house.

At 10:30 P.M., the lights dimmed, the curtain rose, and out of the darkness, like a strange, winding serpent, came the bluesy sound of Sidney Bechet's clarinet. The melody was haunting, yet beautiful, and the Parisians were stunned. They had never heard this kind of music before—the sweet, lazy strains of Dixie—and from that moment on, *La Revue Nègre* was a total triumph.

The biggest success of the evening, however, was Baker's Charleston. Her vibrant dancing startled and amazed the French audience. She was like an unleashed animal, pouncing at audience members, catching them by surprise. As the orchestra gathered momentum, a group of bandanna-clad mammies joined Baker onstage, swiveling their hips energetically. Mesmerized, the crowd rose to its feet, and when the drummer finally smashed the cymbals, Baker somersaulted offstage to a wave of frantic applause.

Moments later, she reappeared wearing nothing but a skirt of pink feathers. In the heat of the spotlight, her beauty was breathtaking.

"Fabuleux!" people yelled. "Fabulous!"

Seized by the passion of the moment, Baker sprang into the arms of another dancer. Her entire body, she remembered, burned with feverish excitement: "Each time I leaped I seemed to touch the sky and when I regained earth it seemed to be mine alone." When the stagehands finally brought the curtain down, the response was deafening.

Baker had taken Paris by storm. The next morning, the box office was swamped, and for the rest of the show's run, security guards were hired to control members of the audience, who sometimes rushed the stage as Baker was finishing her dance.

One widely respected critic pronounced her "the black Venus." Another wrote that Josephine Baker had shown the French "for the first time that black was beautiful." People began to stop her on the street to ask for her autograph. This proved to be embarrassing: Baker could hardly write her name. When flowers arrived backstage after the show, she struggled to read the simple messages inside.

One critic in Paris dubbed Josephine Baker "the black Venus" after her performance in *La Revue Nègre*. Her style and glamour, epitomized here as she lies on a tiger rug, were a quick hit in the City of Light.

With Paul Colin at her side, Baker was introduced to some of the most interesting people in the city: writers and artists, intellectuals and politicians. She visited art exhibitions, cabarets, museums, and elegant parties. Little by little, she began to learn her way around the vast city.

Baker's scrapbook, meanwhile, quickly filled with newspaper reviews, all of which she studied carefully. She felt her heart quicken whenever she spotted her name in the clutter of unfamiliar words. And in those late fall days of 1925, she spotted it frequently. All of Paris, it seemed, wanted to read about Josephine Baker.

5

A Star in Paris

Josephine Baker quickly created a sensation in Paris. By the middle of October 1925, she had found the fame she had so craved, but it was a fame marked by controversy. A good number of Parisians who came to see "the black Venus" walked out in the middle of her Charleston. They considered her dancing offensive and vulgar. One critic called her performance embarrassingly primitive, the jerky antics of a monkey. These barbs must have hurt the 19-year-old Baker, but, as Caroline Dudley pointed out, most people liked her and that was all that mattered.

As *La Revue Nègre* entered its third triumphant week, Baker began to settle comfortably into her new life. With the money she earned, she bought beautiful clothing and expensive perfumes. Her necklace was the most unusual in Paris: a friendly snake named Kiki, who scared off more than one admirer.

Baker wisely sensed that her pet snake added to her exotic allure, and she soon added other pets to her menagerie: a pig named Albert, a squawking parrot, two rabbits, and a pair of goldfish. She called the pets her children and spoiled them outrageously. Her suite at the Hotel Fournet began to resemble a strange sort of zoo; a glamorous, perfume-scented barnyard. Guests had trouble finding a place to sit, but Baker refused to get rid of the animals. She was having too much fun to care what anyone thought.

Every night, after performing in *La Revue Nègre*, Baker was drawn to the jazz-filled cabarets of Montmartre, a section of Paris known at the time for its wild nightlife. One club she visited frequently was Bricktop's. Ada "Bricktop" Smith, an African-American woman 12 years older than Baker, arrived in Paris in 1924 and opened her Montmartre nightclub the same year. Jazz musician Louis Armstrong, composer Cole Porter, and writers Ernest Hemingway and John Steinbeck were among those who passed through "Brickie's" swinging doors.

Bricktop soon adopted the younger Baker, taking her under her wing and introducing her to the city's tight-knit world of black artists and musicians. Baker's suite at the Hotel Fournet was the scene of many wild parties, with Bricktop pouring the drinks, Baker dancing on the coffee table, and Sidney Bechet blowing the blues on a saxophone until the management pounded on the door.

"Everything was for the moment with Josephine," Bricktop remembered. "She couldn't see past today."

After 10 weeks of sellout performances, *La Revue Nègre* went on tour to Berlin, where Baker's Charleston electrified the Germans. On opening night, the audience was so enthusiastic that Baker was lifted onto the shoulders of several men and carried offstage, applause rocking the Nelson Theatre.

During her brief stay in Berlin, Baker was introduced to Max Reinhardt, at that time the most famous director in Germany and Austria. Reinhardt had seen Baker in *Shuffle Along,* and now, watching her perform again, he asked her to become a student at his acting school. In three years' time, he said, he could turn her into a highly polished comedienne.

Baker was flattered, but she was unable to accept Reinhardt's offer. Unknown to the cast of *La Revue Nègre*, she had already signed a contract to star at the Folies Bergère upon her return to Paris. Though she did not know it at the time, this would prove to be a very smart career move. The Folies Bergère was the world's most celebrated music hall, and its 1926 revue, *La Folie du Jour*, would transform Baker into something more than a star: It would turn her into a living legend.

LA FOLIE DU JOUR

Josephine Baker was only 19 years old when she made her first appearance on the stage of the Folies Bergère. The Paris theater, she later wrote, "had a fountain, a canopy as a sky, and chandeliers to provide the sunlight." One of the most spectacular music halls in the world, the Folies Bergère was an appropriate showcase for the sensationally talented Josephine Baker.

In April 1926, when Baker debuted in *La Folie du Jour*, the Parisian music halls were at the height of their creativity. Nothing could rival them for sheer eye-popping spectacle. Like the Hollywood movie studios of the 1930s, the Folies Bergère specialized in overwhelming glamour and beauty. The finished product, as the director liked to say, was "three enchanting hours of fantasy and beauty and fun, an evening's escape into the land of dream-fulfillment."

During this splashy postwar period, it was not unusual for a Folies production to cost a half-million dollars. Most Parisians agreed, however, that it was money well-spent—especially in 1926, when Baker starred in *La Folie du Jour*.

Her opening-night appearance in that show is still remembered as one of *the* great moments in music hall history. The curtain rose to reveal a steamy jungle setting: kapok trees, a winding river, birdcalls, heavy swinging vines. Native drum-beats could be heard in the distance. Then, high above the stage, Baker made her entrance, crawling backward, catlike, down one of the painted trees. She was not wearing a feathered headdress, like most Folies stars. Springing to the stage, landing on all fours like a panther, Baker was wearing nothing but a skirt of brilliant yellow bananas.

The costume was so striking, so fabulously primitive, the Parisians leapt to their feet and cried out in surprise. The conductor slashed the air with his baton, and with the shouts and the applause ringing in her ears, Baker began to dance, the bananas jumping violently with every choreographed move. It was five minutes of sheer theatrical genius.

Folies Bergère

The Folies Bergère is a Parisian music hall that has provided glamorous and exotic entertainment for more than 130 years. Located in the Ninth Arrondissement of Paris, the hall was originally built to serve as an opera house. It opened in May 1869 as the Folies Trévise, where performances included operettas, popular songs, comic operas, and gymnastics. It was renamed the Folies Bergère in September 1872.

The music hall very quickly became a landmark in Paris, a destination for tourists as well as Parisians. The artist Edward Manet's 1882 painting *A Bar at the Folies Bergère* depicts a young woman standing before a mirror in the hall.

From very early on, the Folies gained a reputation for entertainment that featured elaborate costumes and scantily clad women. In the 1920s, the Folies entertainment focused on exotic cultures and people, one reason for Josephine Baker's extraordinary success from her first appearance there. Clad only in a skirt of bananas, Baker caused a sensation with her exuberant dancing and beauty.

The success of the Folies Bergère inspired many imitators, including the Lido and Moulin Rouge in Paris and the *Ziegfeld Follies* in the United States. But from the 1890s to the 1920s, the performers at the Folies Bergère became celebrities, enjoying a fame that they might not have found anywhere else.

Male dancers at the Folies Bergère in Paris surround Josephine Baker. Her opening night appearance in the Folies Bergère's 1926 revue is legendary in music hall history. She came out wearing a skirt made only of yellow bananas.

An hour later, Baker returned and, wearing a grass skirt, she performed the Charleston on a polished mirror, her knees twisting in and out in a dizzying blur. The banana dance, though, was what fascinated everyone. When it was over, Baker threw up her arms and, with a breathtaking leap, landed on top of an artificial palm tree. Panting, she grinned and rolled her eyes at the audience.

The applause was shattering. The Parisians had never witnessed anything like it—certainly never at the Folies Bergère. They rushed into the aisles as the curtain came ringing down.

"Encore! Encore!"

The shouting reached a frenzy, and Baker was forced to return. With a beautiful blue spotlight fixed upon her, she took 12 curtain calls. The young American from St. Louis, Missouri, had been onstage for only a few minutes, but she had won herself a lifetime of fame and admiration.

Wherever Baker went now, photographers hurried after her. Reporters scribbled down her every comment. Fashion designers delivered armloads of beautiful dresses to her apartment on the rue Beaujon. Josephine Baker dolls appeared on the streets of Paris, each wearing a little skirt of bananas. In one fell swoop, she had become the most famous woman in the city.

Young Parisiennes began to copy Baker's closely cut hair, which, from a distance, looked as if it was tarred to her head. "Are you a boy or a girl?" people frequently asked. In response, Baker just smiled.

The chocolate color of her skin became all the rage, and thousands of women smeared themselves with walnut oil and sunbathed for hours to look like the "Black Pearl of the Folies Bergère."

Night after night, different men took Baker out on the town, showering her with expensive gifts: pearls, diamonds, 14-carat-gold fingernail polish, imported flower baskets, rings, bracelets, perfumes. On her twentieth birthday, one admirer gave her a new car.

"She is all but the dictator of Paris," one reviewer noted. Famed artist Pablo Picasso, for whom Baker posed, had a different way of putting it. He likened her to the most glamorous queen of ancient Egypt: "She is the Nefertiti of now."

Baker had arrived in Paris at a time when anything associated with black culture was in vogue, and she contributed to this enthusiastic embrace. Primitive art, African dance, the hot new sounds of American jazz—all were feverishly embraced by the Parisians. Though she had never been anywhere near Africa, Josephine Baker seemed to capture the beauty of the jungle. Exotic and passionately alive, she was, in the words of one poet, "a mysteriously unkillable Something."

FAME AND FORTUNE

Fame came quickly to Baker, and wealth soon followed. By the fall of 1926, only a few months after her scintillating opening-night performance in *La Folie du Jour*, Baker was making more money than any other entertainer in Europe. Nearly 1,000 marriage proposals arrived in the mail and, to Baker's surprise, she became one of the most photographed women in the world. Her lively Charleston was filmed and shown in theaters all over the United States. Back in St. Louis, Carrie and Arthur Martin were stunned by Tumpie's far-reaching success.

The publicity focused not only on Baker herself, but also on her lifestyle, including her exotic pets. There were few sights in Paris more extraordinary than that of La Bakaire, as the French often called her, strolling down the Champs-Élysées with her golden-eyed leopard Chiquita, wearing a diamond collar, on one side and Ethel, a chimpanzee, on the other, a choker around her neck and diamond bracelets dangling from her wrists.

On December 10, 1926, Baker opened her own nightclub on the rue Fontaine. The cabaret, Chez Joséphine, was an immediate success, attracting Parisians and visiting Americans. Albert, her freshly perfumed pet pig, wandered among the tables as Baker entertained the customers with high kicks and witty jokes. Ethel the chimp wore the most stylish hats and tried to catch Baker's feathers as they flew through the air. The customers loved it, and the cabaret was packed every night.

Somehow, amid all this excitement, Baker improved her literacy and found time to write her memoirs, a surprising task for someone who was only 20 years old. *Les Mémoires de Joséphine Baker* was published in Paris in 1927. A delightful book, it was filled with everything from reminiscences of St. Louis to soul food recipes to beauty tips. (She recommended, for instance, that women rub strawberries on their cheeks to give them better color.)

Near the end of the book, Baker pondered her future. She would continue to dance—that was certain—but she also wrote that she was tired of being a star. She wanted to get married, settle down, and have children. She wanted a more peaceful existence, a break from the hectic pace of the music hall.

Soon after the book was published, however, Baker signed a contract to appear in the 1927 revue of the Folies Bergère. *Un Vent de Folie* (A Gust of Madness) should have been a tremendous success; instead, it struck the Parisians as flat and predictable. It wasn't that Baker was different—she had as much energy as ever, and her picture was still appearing in all the newspapers. The problem was that Paris was a city constantly looking for new entertainment, and Baker's bananas were no longer novel. She needed something new—something to keep her on the cutting edge of Parisian entertainment.

That summer, Baker was asked to make her first full-length movie, *La Sirène des Tropiques* (The Siren of the Tropics). The story was a silly one, about a West Indian girl who falls in love with a visiting French engineer. The project intrigued Baker, however, and she agreed to star in the silent film.

The decision proved to be a poor one. Baker's charisma and vibrancy did not translate from stage to screen. Baker hated making the movie and found the process boring and tiresome. She was not a bad actress, but the movie was an inadequate vehicle for her talents. When she saw the finished film, she was embarrassed and angry. The film, in her opinion, had been a complete waste of time.

Fortunately, her next project was much more successful: a two-year, 25-country world tour that Baker would look back upon as a turning point in her career.

From the very start, the 1928–1929 tour was filled with excitement and controversy. Baker's bananas, which had become notorious, shocked and delighted all of Europe. Her energetic dancing thrilled audiences and, in country after country, she established herself as one of the most important, most celebrated of all entertainers.

There was one critical factor, though, that Baker had failed to consider when she planned her tour: religion. Many countries on the itinerary were predominantly Catholic, and the clergy regarded Baker as nothing short of the devil in disguise. Her reckless lifestyle, banana skirt, and short hair were all regarded as sinful. Baker was frequently met at train stations by crowds of angry, sign-waving protesters.

The controversy reached its height in the Austrian city of Vienna. The idea of racial superiority, which would become a basic principle of the Nazis, who took control of Austria in 1938, was popular among the Viennese. It was easy for them to believe that Josephine Baker, a black dancer who lived in Paris, was an inferior being, unfit to take her place in society with civilized white people.

As expected, protests greeted Baker's arrival at the train station. As she was being driven to her hotel in a horse-drawn carriage, the entire city reverberated with the frantic pealing of bells. The churches were warning the citizens that Baker had arrived. At St. Paul's, Masses were held for the salvation of her soul.

As public protest continued to swell, the city council, fearing a riot, refused to let Baker perform until it could determine if she presented any danger to the people of Vienna. A month later, the Austrian Parliament decided that she could appear at the Johann Strauss Theater. The churches were packed that afternoon, as clergymen branded Baker a savage, a decadent heathen determined to corrupt their fine city. The Viennese listened, fascinated, and after the services were over, they rushed home, changed into their evening clothes, and hurried to the theater. They wanted to find out for themselves just how evil Josephine Baker was.

As always, Baker was capable of astonishing, even shocking, an audience—giving the people a performance quite different from what they had come to expect. When Baker walked onstage, she was dressed not in ostrich feathers or bananas but in a beautiful cream-colored gown, buttoned at the neck. The audience gasped. Surely this could not be the woman about whom they had been warned? Baker ignored the excited whispers and began to sing a soft lullaby, "Pretty Little Baby." Outside, she could hear the rhythmic chanting of student radicals. The drama of the moment was unforgettable.

As soon as Baker finished the song, the audience members rose to their feet, cheering and shouting. Waves of applause rushed over the young star. With that one tender song, she had conquered Vienna.

After three weeks of sellout performances, the tour continued on and again encountered trouble. In Prague, Czechoslovakia, Baker found herself caught in the middle of a riot when she arrived at the train station. This time, however, the crowd was made up of overexcited fans, not protesters. Several train windows were shattered, and a half-dozen people were injured. Seeking safety, Baker climbed onto the roof of a nearby limousine. As the car inched its way through the densely packed streets, she waved happily to the enthusiastic crowd.

Violence seemed to follow Baker wherever she went. In Budapest, the capital of Hungary, she was shocked when student protesters threw ammonia bombs onto the stage during her performance. Another evening, a young fan, hopelessly

Carrying one of her many pets, Josephine Baker is shown in Germany during her 1928–1929 tour. In conservative countries like Austria and Argentina, her performances caused some outcry—until she won over audiences.

in love with Baker, shot himself after one of her concerts. In Munich, Germany, the police refused to let her perform, fearing that the show would cause public disorder.

Baker traveled to Spain, where she learned to dance the vigorous *zapateado* and the thunderous, foot-stamping flamenco. In the mountain province of Huesca, she watched in surprise as the cheering audience hurled hundreds of shoes and hats onto the stage. She was later told that this was their way of welcoming her to their city.

Finally, in the summer of 1929, she sailed for South America. Arriving in the Argentine capital of Buenos Aires, she learned that the papers were full of scandalous stories about her. Even President Hipólito Irigoyen had denounced her in the press.

On opening night, hundreds of irate protesters gathered in front of the theater. The atmosphere was extremely tense, and the moment Baker appeared onstage, firecrackers began to explode under the seats. People jumped up, screaming. The musicians immediately started to play a loud tango, hoping to drown out the noise, but they were drowned out by hysterical Argentines, who were yelling and shaking their fists in the air.

The concert was delayed for nearly a half-hour while the police dragged the most violent agitators from the hall. The smell of gunpowder was still fresh in the air when Baker began her show. It was a nerve-racking experience for everyone.

The rest of the South American engagements went more smoothly. Nevertheless, Baker felt relieved when she played the last city on the tour. She was eager to return to Paris. She was tired of demonstrations and trains and ships and strange hotel rooms. She was ready to settle down. Her only fear was that the Parisians might have forgotten her after two years and that she would have to prove herself all over again.

6

Follies

Josephine Baker was quite serious about her desire to settle down. When she finally returned to Paris in late 1929, she bought a spectacular new home in the lovely suburb of Le Vésinet, 45 minutes from Paris. Her new home, Le Beau-Chêne (Beautiful Oak), was a 30-room mansion with a handsome gravel drive-way, a stately parade of sturdy oaks, and a magnificent garden. Baker immediately began to plant rows of carrots, cabbage, and black-eyed peas. A short distance from the house, she built a large pool surrounded by marble columns and statues of Roman goddesses. On hot days, she floated nude among the water lilies, giving press interviews and chatting casually with the neighbors.

It was a heady time for Baker, and she enjoyed the opportunity to indulge herself. She was earning enough money to support an extravagant lifestyle. At a time when many Americans were beginning to experience the first hardships of the Great Depression, Baker was worth more than one million dollars.

Her career continued to prosper, the result of good luck and shrewd decisions. During this period, Baker began a long and successful collaboration with the Casino de Paris. The Casino was not as famous as the Folies Bergère, but it was still a first-class music hall. Its seasonal productions were extremely lavish, and in no time, Baker re-established herself as the leading star of the Parisian stage.

Her happiest moments, though, were spent at Le Beau-Chêne. To her neighbors' surprise, Baker made a real effort to become part of the community. One by one, she got to know the local people, and whenever she heard that a family could not pay its coal bill, she quietly took care of the matter herself.

Baker also became involved in the affairs of the local orphanage. She took an active interest in the children; her ever-growing collection of animals delighted the youngsters, and their frequent visits to the house brought her a great deal of joy.

Baker would later look back on these years with affection. At home, she was surrounded by love; at the theater, she continued to meet the most celebrated people in Europe. The noted physicist Albert Einstein came backstage one evening and complimented Baker on her performance. The king of Siam was so excited by her dancing that he offered her one of his prized elephants (one of the few animals she ever refused to accept). A particularly happy memory was the evening Noble Sissle appeared at her dressing-room door. The two spent several delightful hours reminiscing about the *Shuffle Along* days.

In 1933, Baker was back on tour again, performing in England, Scandinavia, Belgium, Greece, Italy, and Egypt. The response was tremendous in every country. In Copenhagen, the leading newspaper called Baker "the most fantastic show lady" ever to play the Danish city. In the opera capital of Parma, Italy, the crowd wept at her moving performance of the song "Haiti." The next morning, the enormous one-word headline said it all: DIVINA (DIVINE).

The following year, Baker surprised everyone by starring not at the Casino but in a revival of *La Créole*, a frothy operetta written by French composer Jacques Offenbach. At first, Baker was afraid she would be unable to sing the demanding role of the West Indian girl. Classical music, after all, was hardly her area of expertise. The challenge proved irresistible, however, and Baker managed to turn in a delightful performance. *La Créole* became so popular, in fact, that on one occasion it was transmitted by radio to England. "How incredible to think that my voice had crossed the Channel!" Baker later wrote.

But her career would not be limited to the two sides of the English Channel. Baker was invited to travel to New York to appear in the 1936 version of the *Ziegfeld Follies*. Florenz Ziegfeld, the legendary theatrical producer, had died in 1932, and the New York show was now being produced by Jake and Lee Shubert. Like all the *Ziegfeld Follies*, the 1936 production promised to be spectacular: Vincente Minnelli was designing the sets and costumes, Ira Gershwin was writing the lyrics, Vernon Duke was writing the score, and the popular comedienne Fanny Brice would be the headliner. Two other cast members, Bob Hope and Eve Arden, would go on to be major stars. Clearly, Baker was in good company.

Baker had mixed feelings about returning to the United States after 10 years, but she thought that it would advance her career and establish her as a true international star. Additionally, she saw the *Follies* as an opportunity to further the black cause. By appearing onstage with Fanny Brice, she hoped to prove to American audiences that it did not matter if a person was black or white—what mattered was talent, not skin color.

It was a noble ambition, but one that would soon lead to bitter disappointment. Ten years and several thousand miles separated the 29-year-old entertainer from her native country; apparently, she had forgotten how deeply the roots of discrimination were embedded in American society.

RETURN TO AMERICA

In September 1935, Baker boarded the French ocean liner *Normandie* for New York. Later, she would claim that Ziegfeld's widow, film star Billie Burke, happened to be on the same voyage. According to Baker, she sent Burke an invitation to have dinner together. When Burke made her appearance in the large dining room, however, she stared at Baker coldly, turned on her heel, and left without a word. Baker interpreted it as racial discrimination, and it would prove to be merely the first in a series of cruel moments that poisoned Baker's return to the United States.

Upon arriving in New York City, she checked into the Hotel St. Moritz, where the manager told Baker that she would have to use the servants' entrance because of her skin color. The fact that Baker was a *Follies* star made no difference. Many of the guests were from the South, the manager explained, and the sight of an African-American woman in the lobby might offend them. The situation was embarrassing, but Baker decided not to make a fuss. She knew it would be bad publicity for the show.

Before her rehearsals began, Baker was able to spend five days visiting her family in St. Louis. Since her departure in 1925, Grandma McDonald and Arthur Martin had died. Arthur's last few years had been tragic. His fierce temper and frequent bouts of depression finally resulted in mental illness. Carrie had him committed to the city asylum, where he died in 1934.

After leaving St. Louis, Baker made a quick visit to Chicago, where she told her husband, Willie Baker, that she wanted a divorce. Josephine and Willie were strangers by now; they had not seen each other in 10 years, and both agreed that it was foolish to continue the marriage. After signing the necessary papers, Josephine hurried back to New York, where rehearsals for the *Follies* were under way.

Sadly, the next few weeks were the most discouraging of Baker's professional career. Not only did the stars ignore her, but the *Follies* management treated her like a child, insisting that they knew what was best for her. Baker tried to stay agreeable, but her mood turned sour when she realized she had only a small role in the show. Fanny Brice was given all the best scenes, and Bob Hope, a former boxer, was allowed to introduce the show's most memorable song, "I Can't Get Started With You." Baker, on the other hand, appeared onstage only four times.

What angered her most, though, was that she was not allowed to wear the outfits she had brought with her from Paris. Vincente Minnelli's costumes were undeniably beautiful, but they were not the costumes Baker wanted to wear. One creation, a gold mesh evening gown, weighed nearly 100 pounds. It was stunning to see, but impossible to perform in.

"I could tell from the start that I'd never make it," Baker wrote. "I had been overglamorized, hopelessly typecast."

She was not surprised, therefore, when the critics panned her opening-night performance. Her voice, they said, was too thin and "dwarf-like" to fill the spacious Winter Garden Theatre. It confused and annoyed New Yorkers to hear an African-American woman speak with a French accent, and Baker was immediately labeled a "foreigner." Even her celebrated banana dance fell flat. *Time* magazine was unusually harsh, dismissing the "Negro wench ... whose dancing and singing might be topped practically anywhere outside of Paris."

Praise was lavished, however, on Fanny Brice, Bob Hope, Eve Arden, and especially Vincente Minnelli. It disappointed and angered Baker that she could not share in their success. She eventually told Jake and Lee Shubert that she wanted to leave

Josephine Baker performs "The Conga" during the *Ziegfeld Follies* at the Winter Garden Theatre in New York. Her appearance in the *Ziegfeld Follies* in 1936 was disastrous, and she asked to be let out of her contract early.

the *Follies,* and being smart businessmen, they quickly released her from her contract. She was replaced by the burlesque star Gypsy Rose Lee.

Sadder but wiser, Baker returned to France, where she headlined the 1937 revue of the Folies Bergère, *En Super Folies.* She also reopened her cabaret, Chez Joséphine, spending her midnights singing and dancing for the crowds of tourists who attended the 1937 Colonial Exposition. The situation was ironic: The Americans who had disliked her at home could not seem to get enough of her in Paris. Increasingly, Baker felt that she and the United States were simply not compatible, and not long after her return to Paris, she legally became a French citizen. Now, she felt, she truly belonged.

Her happiness at being back in France increased in early 1937, when Baker fell in love with a handsome Jewish millionaire named Jean Lion. Ambitious and clever, Lion had made his fortune in the sugar market, and his good looks and sophisticated charm dazzled Baker. In turn, her energy and exuberant personality impressed him. Even more impressive to him was Baker's popularity with the French people. At age 27, Lion was considering a career in politics, and he sensed immediately that a woman like Baker could open many doors for him.

Baker and Lion shared a passion for outdoor sports. In the spring of 1937, they filled their days with horseback riding, fox hunting, sightseeing, and racing through the French countryside in expensive automobiles. They even flew airplanes together, a sport that obsessed Baker. Whenever she had an hour to spare, she rushed to the airport and, in no time, was doing loops over the Palace of Versailles.

During one such plane ride, in fact, Lion proposed to Baker. She accepted immediately. At 31, she feared that her youth was passing, and with it her chances of raising a family. A new career as Madame Lion would not only be secure but wonderfully romantic—or so Baker believed. Like many stars, she had convinced herself that what she really wanted was a quiet life out of the spotlight. She did not realize how important fame had become to her.

UNTRADITIONAL WIFE

The wedding was held that fall in Lion's hometown of Crève-coeur-le-Grand, a village northwest of Paris. On the day of the ceremony, hundreds of people filled the square. After Baker and

Lion exchanged their vows, cheers went up, trumpets sounded, and shotguns were fired ceremoniously into the air. Baker was thrilled. "I want to be a housewife and have at least six children," she told the press, a plan that her husband supported wholeheartedly.

Baker was undoubtedly speaking from the heart and, if she had been willing to sacrifice her career, her third marriage might have lasted. Instead, it was doomed from the start. In his own way, Lion was a celebrity in Parisian society, a handsome playboy who was not used to sharing the spotlight. Now that he and Baker were married, he expected her to become a traditional wife. As an aristocrat, he relied upon her to plan dinner parties, write tasteful thank-you notes, and arrange charity teas. In public, Baker was expected to be well-dressed, well-read, and well-spoken. In short, her job was to make her husband look powerful and successful.

Baker had enjoyed a glamorous career, and she was not suited to the role of trophy wife. She tried her best to become a society hostess, but she never felt comfortable. She was used to having people surround *her*, and the idea of existing for someone else was not entirely pleasant. Baker respected and loved Lion, but she was not willing to become his shadow. Naturally, this created tension between them. Also, with Baker's hectic schedule, she and her husband were not able to spend as much time together as they would have liked. He worked during the day; she worked at night.

Finally, Lion asked her to quit show business. Baker knew it was the only way she could save her marriage and, hoping to begin a family, she agreed to retire. First, however, she insisted on a farewell tour. Lion grudgingly gave his approval.

The tour was difficult in more ways than one. The atmosphere in Europe in the late 1930s was becoming increasingly tense. Adolf Hitler seized power in Germany in 1933, and by 1935 his plans to establish the German people as the "master race" were beginning to take shape. Claiming to be a man of

Josephine Baker danced with her husband, Jean Lion, during a "Ski Night" held at the Porte de Versailles in Paris in 1937. Throughout her short marriage to Lion, Baker was torn between her desire to settle down and her desire to perform.

peace, Hitler was in reality a ruthless dictator determined to create a new world order. He despised the Soviet system of bolshevism, considered France an enemy, and regarded all Jewish people as evil. His book *Mein Kampf* (My Struggle) was the bible of the growing Nazi Party.

As the rest of Europe watched apprehensively, Germany allied itself with Italy in 1936. Later, it did the same with Japan. The real aggression began in 1938, when Hitler's troops occupied Austria. Baker was just beginning her farewell tour at that time, and the increasing rumors of war deeply worried her. What if the Nazis invaded France? As a black French citizen and the wife of a Jew, she knew she would be in great danger.

Lion accompanied her on the early part of the tour, but business concerns eventually took him back to France, where the government situation was very shaky. Baker continued the tour alone and, with every passing week, she realized how much she truly loved to perform. She felt most alive when she was onstage, basking in the admiration of excited crowds. Berlin, Warsaw, Nice, Zurich, London ... the longer the tour lasted, the more reluctant she was to go home.

Finally, Lion lost his temper. He demanded that Baker abandon her career and return to Paris. Not surprisingly, she refused. Baker now had to make an extremely difficult decision. She still loved her husband, but after a great deal of soul-searching, she had to admit that she loved her career more. At this time, she discovered she was pregnant. She continued the tour, however, and was beginning to knit a colorful collection of baby clothes when she suffered a sudden miscarriage.

"I lost the only thing that could have bound Jean and me together," Baker wrote. After less than a year of marriage, the Lions decided to separate.

Meanwhile, the wheels of war were beginning to turn faster. One of Hitler's basic beliefs was that the Jews were an impure people who poisoned the Aryan race. He felt they must be dealt with sharply, and on November 9, 1938, the shops and homes of Jewish families throughout Germany were attacked and burned to the ground. Thousands of windows were shattered as chanting Nazi youths ran through the streets. The Night of Broken Glass, as it came to be called, shocked all of Europe. When Baker heard of the persecution and the rioting, she quickly joined the International League Against Racism and Anti-Semitism.

Less than 10 months later, on September 1, 1939, Hitler's troops invaded Poland. Great Britain and France immediately issued declarations of war. World War II had begun.

7

The Resistance

Like many Europeans, Josephine Baker was inspired to volunteer to help the war effort. She chose to join the Red Cross, where the need for volunteers was great. The woman who had once been the toast of Paris spent several hours every day at the busy Red Cross center, putting together boxes of food, finding housing for homeless families, and ladling out soup for the lines of hungry people. In the evenings, when she was not performing with entertainer Maurice Chevalier at the Casino de Paris, she appeared at charity functions, always ready to sing and dance to raise money for the war effort.

In the spring of 1940, the war began to escalate. On April 9, Hitler's troops occupied the neutral territories of Norway and Denmark, and there was widespread fear that Germany might invade France next. "It became the custom to bolt the shutters and to black out the lights, and everyone got used to waiting," Chevalier wrote.

The Casino de Paris closed at the end of May. Baker pushed herself harder than ever, spending six days a week at the Red Cross center. On the seventh day, she flew much-needed supplies across the border to Belgium. It did not take long for her patriotism to attract the notice of the French military police. One of its top officers, Jacques Abtey, quietly visited Baker at Le Beau-Chêne; he wanted to know if she would be willing to become an undercover agent. Baker was surprised, and deeply honored, to receive such an invitation.

Abtey's reason for approaching Baker was simple. As a well-known entertainer, she had access to important people and could come and go as she pleased. As long as she was discreet, she would not be suspected. Baker knew that the job could be dangerous, but she assured Abtey that she was prepared to give her life for her adopted country. In France, she explained, she had discovered the meaning of true freedom, and she would do anything to protect it.

In this way, Josephine Baker became a member of the French Resistance. Less is known about Baker's wartime activities than about any other part of her life. She herself was always reluctant to discuss this period; even 30 years after the war ended, she still felt the need to be discreet.

After being recruited into the secret organization, Baker was put through a series of rigorous tests to train her for whatever she might encounter on a mission. She learned how to handle a pistol and within weeks was able to shoot the flame of a candle at 20 yards. She learned karate. She was drilled in German and Italian until she could speak and read both languages comfortably. She was also put through a series of challenging memory tests. As Abtey explained, there would be instances when she would have to remember information for weeks, even months, at a time.

Finally, at the end of her training, Baker was given a handful of cyanide pills. Abtey told her that if she ever found herself in a situation she could not handle, the capsules killed instantly. Suicide, the Resistance believed, was a noble alternative to enemy capture.

Baker's first assignment was accomplished with surprising ease. As a popular entertainer, she was on friendly terms with several high-ranking officials in the Italian government, including Benito Mussolini, the ruler of Italy. Within a matter of days, she successfully obtained some valuable information—possibly a codebook—that she passed on to Abtey.

Baker's career as an undercover agent had just begun when the Germans occupied Paris on June 13, 1940. Along with thousands of other terrified citizens, Baker fled the city, which fell to the enemy without a single shot being fired. Nazi flags unfurled triumphantly from the windows as German troops marched in front of the Eiffel Tower.

"Those who stayed in the city lived in a kind of nightmare," Maurice Chevalier remembered. "We just tried to hang on and do our job the best we could."

Baker had no desire to collaborate with an occupying army. She drove south as quickly as she could, heading not to Le Beau-Chêne, which was too close to occupied Paris, but to Les Milandes, a spacious 50-room chateau she had rented in 1938. Baker had fallen in love with the house the moment she saw it, but she had never been able to spend more than a few days there. Much later, Les Milandes would play a significant role

IN HER OWN WORDS...

When Josephine Baker and Jacques Abtey met at Le Beau-Chêne, she talked about herself and her feelings toward the French. According to *Jazz Cleopatra: Josephine Baker in Her Time* by Phyllis Rose, Baker told Abtey:

France made me what I am. I will be grateful forever. The people of Paris have given me everything. They have given me their hearts, and I have given them mine. I am ready, Captain, to give them my life.

in her life. In the summer of 1940, however, she saw it as little more than a safe refuge from the Nazis.

CELEBRITY AND SPY

In July, Abtey joined Baker at the chateau, and together they spent the next few months hiding nervous refugees and listening to uncertain reports over the radio. In this way, they learned that the Germans had occupied only part of France. There were now two zones, the northern and the southern, the second of which was still held by the French. No one could say how long this division would last.

As fall approached, Baker continued to shelter as many people as she could, but the situation was risky. Anyone sympathetic to the Nazis could turn her in for a hefty reward. She was relieved, therefore, when she and Abtey received orders from Resistance headquarters to travel to the neutral territory of Lisbon, Portugal. There, Abtey would make contact with members of British intelligence.

For the next eight months, Baker and Abtey worked tirelessly for the French Resistance. Their assignments were difficult, and often dangerous, but they were very successful. As Abtey had hoped, Baker was able to travel across borders easily—something he would have had trouble doing on his own. Whenever anyone asked why she was traveling so much, Baker gave the simple excuse that she was on tour. To make the ruse look legitimate, she brought along many pieces of luggage and a colorful assortment of pets, including two monkeys and a Great Dane. Abtey, carefully disguised, was usually introduced as her secretary.

Baker's "tour" was exciting, exotic, and exhausting. Even after coming down with pneumonia, she refused to let herself rest. Lisbon, Marseilles, London, Algiers, Barcelona, Madrid—in every city, Baker was invited to embassy functions and high-society parties. Because these events were usually filled with government officials, she attended them all, eavesdropping on

Josephine Baker received the insignia of sublieutenant in the Women's Auxiliary of the French Air Force during World War II. As an entertainer, Baker was able to travel more freely during the war, allowing her to collect and transport vital information for the French Resistance.

the conversations around her. Later, locked in her hotel room, she carefully wrote down all she had heard, her invisible-ink pen racing across her sheet music.

As a celebrity, Baker was rarely subjected to border searches—more often than not, she and Abtey were simply waved through customs. They were able to collect a good deal of valuable information for the French Resistance.

In June 1941, however, Baker's luck ran out. She developed an infection and, because she was still recovering from pneumonia, her condition swiftly turned critical. Years later, she would claim that the Nazis had poisoned her with cyanide. In any event, her illness was so serious that she had to spend the next 21 months slowly recovering in Casablanca, a port city in Morocco.

At first, when Baker appeared to be making little, if any, progress in her recovery, Abtey stayed by her side constantly. Concerned friends visited her daily at the Mers Sultan clinic. Many of these visitors were Resistance members, and secret meetings were frequently held at her bedside. Usually, Baker was too weak to follow the hushed conversations.

As time went on, a painful case of peritonitis set in. Blood poisoning followed, and no less than three operations were performed to save Baker's life. For months, she remained delirious, her body shaking with fever. The rumor soon spread that she had died, and her obituary promptly appeared in newspapers throughout the world.

It was not until March 1943 that Baker felt strong enough to leave the hospital. The war was still going on and, to her dismay, Germany now occupied all of France. It did not appear that the fighting would end anytime soon.

Before leaving Casablanca, Baker was invited to perform at the Liberty Club, a canteen where black and white soldiers could mingle socially. It had been two years since Baker last appeared onstage, but knowing how much the concert would mean to the men, she accepted the invitation. Hundreds of American soldiers turned out; many could not fit inside the canteen and scrambled onto the roof to hear the music through the air vents.

That appearance at the Liberty Club was a dramatic moment in Baker's career. She looked extremely thin and her stomach was still swathed in bandages, but she had lost none of her old enthusiasm. As she entertained the men with a Gershwin tune, she felt a wonderful energy filling her body. The 20 minutes Baker spent onstage were more beneficial to her recovery than the interminable months she had spent in the hospital. When the concert ended, the soldiers jumped to their feet, cheering and applauding loudly. It was one of the warmest, most excit- ing ovations Baker had ever received, and it helped determine her future participation in the war.

Baker told Abtey that she wanted to go on tour again—a real tour, this time. Her performance at the canteen had convinced her that the Allied soldiers desperately needed entertainment. Naturally, her doctors discouraged the idea, but Baker's mind was made up. She would do all she could to help the Allied forces. Anything less, she felt, would be unpatriotic.

Abtey agreed to accompany her, and within weeks the details had been arranged. Baker was on the road again, only

Berthe Fraser

There were many courageous women who, like Baker, chose to join the French Resistance when German troops swept over the border during World War II. One of the most inspiring is Berthe Fraser.

Fraser was a 40-year-old housewife who was living in the town of Arras, France, when World War II began. Her husband was British, and when soldiers (many serving as spies) began to arrive in France from England in 1940, Fraser created an underground movement that helped smuggle the British pilots and spies to the coast. There, they would be hidden and then transported back to England. She had successfully saved dozens of British soldiers in this way when, in 1941, she was betrayed and arrested by the Gestapo, which was the Nazi secret police. Fraser was sent to prison in Belgium for 15 months, before finally being released in December 1942.

Immediately after her release, Fraser resumed her underground activity, supplying Allied soldiers in France with a network of support. She arranged for safe hiding places, shelter, and transportation. She coordinated meetings, carried messages, and even served as a courier, traveling on foot or by car with critical documents, weapons, or even dynamite needed for sabotage efforts.

In February 1944, Fraser was again betrayed, this time by a British agent she had helped. The Gestapo arrested her and tortured her for 28 days, trying to force her to give up the names of contacts and other valuable information. She spent more than six months in solitary confinement, without giving up any information. Fraser was sentenced to death and was awaiting her execution when American and British troops stormed her prison on September 1, 1944. After her release, she received many honors, including the Croix de Guerre, the American Medal of Freedom, and a letter of gratitude from General Dwight D. Eisenhower.

this time there was one stipulation: Wherever she performed, she insisted that the black soldiers be allowed to sit with the whites. Usually, blacks were forced to stand in the back, a custom Baker tried to abolish.

In 1943, this simple request was considered controversial. The U.S. Army, which was segregated according to race, bristled at the idea of a black woman trying to change its long-standing policy. Nevertheless, Baker believed it was absolutely necessary that blacks and whites be treated equally in the army. She saw no point in waging war against Hitler if discrimination was allowed to exist on the battlefield.

Not every U.S. Army official agreed with Baker, but she was usually given her way. It was a small, but significant, step forward in the fight against racism.

PERFORMING FOR THE TROOPS

For the next year and a half, Baker entertained American, British, and French forces throughout North Africa and the Middle East. As usual, she drove herself to the point of exhaustion, never complaining and never accepting any pay for her work. She saw herself as simply another soldier doing her duty for her country.

The conditions under which Baker performed were far from luxurious, and frequently dangerous. Material for clothing was hard to come by during the war, and many of Baker's costumes were hastily assembled from pieces of spare cloth. She rarely performed in theaters, usually singing and dancing on a few boards stretched across empty oil drums. Evening performances were lit by military searchlights. More than once, Baker had to drop to the stage in the middle of a song as German aircraft appeared overhead, spraying bullets into the crowd.

Traveling from one military camp to another presented its own difficulties. Maps were unreliable, the heat could be excruciating, violent sandstorms made progress slow, and fresh water was scarce. Sleeping was often impossible: The night air was extremely cold, and sand fleas infested the bedrolls.

Starving jackals and coyotes were a constant menace. Baker never lost her courage, however, keeping up her spirits wherever she went. To the French soldiers stationed in the searing Libyan desert, she was like an uncorked bottle of champagne, bubbling and exotic. When she danced the Charleston, it was a delightful reminder of prewar Paris. When she sang "La Marseillaise," the French national anthem, it was a sobering reminder of the ongoing struggle for liberty. The men cheered themselves hoarse at every performance.

By mid-1944, the Allies appeared to be winning the war. A disgraced Mussolini had resigned as the leader of Italy, Allied bombs were raining down upon Germany, and Hitler's efforts to occupy Russia had failed. On June 6, the Americans and the British invaded France, and by August, Paris was liberated. People wept joyfully as the Allied soldiers rode through the crowded streets.

Baker returned home, but stayed only long enough to reorganize the tour, which would focus on countries that had been liberated. Leaving Paris, she took with her a French bandleader she had met in the early 1930s, Jo Bouillon. Together they performed at many benefits, raising more than a million francs for war victims. Bouillon's admiration for Baker grew steadily as he watched her tour the army camps and visit the hospitals, comforting the wounded. He was especially moved when she distributed Christmas presents to the poor—gifts she had bought by pawning her jewelry.

By April 1945, Germany was on the brink of collapse. Italy had long since surrendered to the Allies, the British were sweeping across northern Germany, and the Russians had surrounded the capital city of Berlin. Hitler, in his desperation, realized that he had been defeated, and on April 30, he committed suicide in his Berlin bunker.

Josephine Baker joked around with a soldier as she entertained troops in 1945 during a victory party in London. For the last two years of World War II, she performed for Allied troops across North Africa and the Middle East. She insisted that black soldiers be allowed to sit with white soldiers during her shows.

After nearly six years, the European war was over. Baker and Jo Bouillon were on tour when the good news was announced, and they made arrangements to return to Paris as quickly as possible. As their ship made its way toward France, Baker began to think about her future. Now that the war was over, there was no longer any need to entertain the troops. Her career as a Resistance agent was also finished.

Bouillon suggested that Baker go on tour again. It was an idea for which the 38-year-old entertainer felt little enthusiasm. Somehow, she felt she should do something more significant, more valuable than simply accepting another round of concert engagements. During the war, Baker had discovered a deep need within herself to help other people. She did not see how she could satisfy this need by dancing in bananas again.

The tour was arranged, however, and Baker spent the early months of 1946 appearing in major cities across Europe and North Africa. In every country, she was as popular as ever. Yet, she still felt the need to do something more important, more lasting.

That summer, while performing in Casablanca, a sharp pain seized her stomach. Within hours, Baker was seriously ill. Two emergency operations were performed, and to her deep disappointment she again found herself confined to the hospital.

Baker was still in her sickbed, in fact, when the French government presented her with the distinguished Medal of the Resistance with Rosette for her patriotism during the war. As the medal was pinned to her hospital gown that October afternoon, she felt extremely proud and, at the same time, a little wistful. She wondered if she would ever again find another cause that would give her the satisfaction and pride she had known during the war.

8

Challenging Discrimination

Battling illness, Josephine Baker was eventually able to recover enough strength to make the journey back to Paris. She believed that the more experienced doctors there would be able to cure her. But postwar conditions in Paris were grim. Doctors were busy with victims of the war, and medicine was difficult to obtain. For several months, Baker's condition remained serious. Every day, Jo Bouillon visited her at the hospital, anxiously watching for signs of improvement. He could see that Baker had lost a great deal of weight; she looked thin and worn out in her hospital gown. Her spirit remained undiminished, however. She saw her illness as a challenge, not a defeat.

Gradually and slowly, Baker began to recover. She gained strength, and her appetite increased. As she started to feel healthier, Baker's thoughts turned to her future. Bouillon would spend hours by her bedside, listening to her discuss her hopes and dreams. Her first and most important goal was to raise a family. At age 40, Baker knew her childbearing years were coming to an end. Adoption, therefore, was the logical solution. As soon as she was well, she hoped to visit the local orphanages.

Jo Bouillon also had dreams. A talented bandleader, he had just been appointed director of a popular cabaret in Paris. Thanks to his radio program, his name was becoming well known in the city's music circles. Soon, his dreams began to include plans for a future with Baker. By the spring of 1947, the couple had fallen in love. When Bouillon asked for her hand in marriage, Baker happily agreed. After the confusion of the war, she was eager to settle down and begin raising a family.

One sunny afternoon, Baker and Bouillon drove to Les Milandes, the fifteenth-century chateau where she and Jacques Abtey spent the early months of 1940 hiding refugees. The castle-like home was in the Dordogne Valley, a beautiful, rocky region in the southern part of France.

For hours, Baker poked through the drafty rooms and wandered through the overgrown garden. Nearby, the Dordogne River wound its lazy way northward. There was a quiet, unhurried feeling to the estate, and by the end of the afternoon, Baker decided that she and Bouillon would raise their adopted children at Les Milandes.

To Baker's delight, the owners were willing to sell the secluded property. To raise the necessary money, Baker sold her five-story townhouse in Paris. She also made arrangements to sell Le Beau-Chêne, her home in Le Vésinet.

As time passed, Baker's plans for the estate began to broaden. Not only did she want to make Les Milandes her home, she hoped to turn it into a tourist resort, a vacation getaway for city dwellers. The setting was rugged and beautiful; to make it even more attractive, she decided to build a swimming pool, a restaurant, and a small zoo.

Baker's plan was charming, but it would take plenty of money to turn the unheated, crumbling chateau into a popular attraction. That meant only one thing: She would have to go on tour again.

Baker and Bouillon were married in the stone chapel at Les Milandes on June 3, 1947. After the simple ceremony, there was singing and dancing and the cutting of a spectacular five-foot wedding cake. Baker was in wonderful spirits that day. It happened to be her forty-first birthday, and she felt tremendously optimistic about the future. If all went well, the profits from her tour would allow construction to begin at Les Milandes before the end of the year.

Unfortunately, the 1947–1948 world tour was extremely rocky. Baker's concerts in Europe and South America were highly successful, but in Havana, Cuba, she encountered a problem. Arriving at the hotel where Bouillon had made their reservations, the couple was told that no rooms were available. Baker immediately suspected she was being turned away because she was black.

Eleven years earlier, when she was forced to use the servants' entrance at a New York hotel, Baker had accepted the situation. Blacks and whites simply did not mix in prewar society. Now, feeling an angry pride rise within her, she decided to fight back. Upon leaving the hotel in Havana, she contacted a lawyer and filed a formal complaint. The local papers, sniffing out the story, requested interviews, which Baker granted. Answering the reporters' questions helped her solidify her ideas about racism.

SPEAKING OUT

Baker stayed in Havana for three months, speaking against discrimination wherever she went. As a well-known entertainer, she had one distinct advantage: Her name could draw a crowd.

Baker's ideas were simple yet effective. She believed that all people were created equal and that blacks and whites could live together peacefully. At public gatherings, she vividly described episodes from her life: the night of terror when Boxcar Town

On her forty-first birthday, Josephine Baker married orchestra leader
Jo Bouillon at Les Milandes, their new home in the Dordogne Valley of
France. Baker planned to raise their adopted children there and turn the
chateau into a tourist attraction as well.

burned; the *Shuffle Along* cast making fun of her because of her dark skin; her arrival in Vienna, the church bells warning the citizens. These memories, and others, gave Baker's speeches a painful urgency that was difficult to ignore. The people of Havana were deeply moved and quickly formed the Association of Friends of Josefina. Its symbol, appropriately, was two hearts intertwined.

By the time Baker left for the United States, her activities in Cuba had been well publicized. One by one, theater owners began to cancel her engagements—she was too political for their tastes. Baker refused to yield to the financial pressure, however. She believed the fight for justice was more important than money. Gradually, she began to see herself as a spokeswoman for all oppressed minorities.

At Fisk University, a black college in Nashville, Tennessee, Baker lectured on the subject of "Racial Equality in France." The students seemed eager to listen, but at the same time they were wary of anyone who tried to change the system, fearful that things might only get worse. This fear, which led to the acceptance of injustice, saddened Baker. Social change, she learned, was a slow and painful process.

In New York City, it was nearly impossible to find a hotel that would allow Baker to stay for more than one night. Again and again, she and Bouillon were told to pack their bags and leave. In effect, Baker was being forced out of the country. Yet there was little she could do to change the situation. This kind of treatment was apparently the bitter price she had to pay for her belief in social change.

Deeply discouraged, Baker returned to France in February 1948. There, she began the enormous task of turning Les Milandes into a tourist center. Hardly taking time to unpack, she began to contact architects, gardeners, electricians, plumbers, and carpenters. Soon, the sleepy chateau was buzzing with activity. Fences were erected, concrete was poured, geraniums were planted, and one by one, Baker's animals began to arrive.

Monkeys, parrots, dogs, cats, mice, peacocks—all found their way to the old chateau in the Dordogne Valley.

The world tour had not raised enough money, so Baker had to continue to make personal appearances. These concert engagements frequently took her out of France, but she did not lose heart. Every appearance, she knew, would bring Les Milandes closer to completion.

After 19 months of work, the chateau was ready for its grand opening on September 4, 1949. The event was well-publicized, and Baker was hoping that at least 1,500 people would attend. She was delighted, and a little stunned, when 10,000 showed up, eager to take part in the celebration. All afternoon, families bowled on the lawn, ran foot-races, visited the animals, relaxed under the trees, rode bicycles, and listened to Baker sing on a little stage in the pleasure garden. As the sun slipped over the horizon and darkness fell, fireworks lit up the sky.

Later, when everyone had gone home and Bouillon had totaled up the receipts, Baker was delighted to see that they had raised more than a quarter of a million francs. Now, they could afford to put in a soccer field and start to dig the swimming pool.

FUNDRAISING TOUR

No matter how much money Baker made, it never seemed to be enough. Her plans to improve the chateau were so costly that touring became a way of life. Switzerland, Spain, Holland, Germany, North Africa—the touring was a vicious cycle. To support Les Milandes, she had to stay on tour, but by doing so, she was rarely able to enjoy what she worked so hard to create.

By 1951, Baker was back in the United States, dazzling audiences with her dramatic singing, sensational dancing, and $150,000 wardrobe. In San Francisco, the critics made no attempt to restrain their enthusiasm; she was, in their opinion, "the most exciting thing to hit [the city] since the Golden Gate Bridge."

But, as always, controversy surrounded Baker's tour. Theater managers were concerned by Baker's reputation for speaking out against discrimination. Several of them decided to cancel her engagements rather than deal with outraged white customers. White supremacist groups like the Ku Klux Klan threatened her on several occasions, but Baker refused to back down. As she explained to the press, she was demanding nothing more than the basic rights "granted to any other citizen of this country."

In Miami, Florida, where discrimination was quietly enforced, Baker was told that African Americans were too afraid to come to the all-white Copa City, where she was scheduled to perform. Faced with this challenge, she spent the next two days driving through the black neighborhoods, assuring the people that they had the right to attend her show.

On opening night, the black community turned out in droves. Seeing so many African Americans sitting in the audience, Baker's eyes grew teary. "I can't express my joy," she told the crowd. "This is a very significant occasion for us, and by 'us' I mean the *entire human race.*"

In city after city, Baker made a point of visiting retail stores, chambers of commerce, and local industries. At each stop, she encouraged employers to hire more African Americans. While in San Francisco, she made an appointment to see Frank Teasdale, the president of the Key System Transit Company in Oakland, California. Their meeting was tense.

"You mean to tell me that Negroes who managed to drive army trucks during the war aren't qualified to drive your city buses?" she asked. Teasdale tried to tell her that the policy was not his to change, but Baker could see she was wasting her time and walked out of the office.

In every theater and nightclub where she performed, Baker made sure that African-American stagehands and musicians were hired. She also refused to accept engagements in any city where African Americans could not stay in the first-class hotels. Atlanta, therefore, was dropped from the itinerary.

In Los Angeles, Baker went so far as to have a Texan arrested for calling her a racial epithet in a restaurant. In court, she insisted her civil rights had been violated. The judge agreed, and the man was fined $100.

The highlight of Baker's tour occurred in New York City on May 20, 1951. On that day, the National Association for the Advancement of Colored People (NAACP) named her the Most Outstanding Woman of the Year and sponsored Josephine Baker Day in Harlem. Despite the wet weather, 100,000 people turned out for the gala event. As the 27-car parade snaked its way down Seventh Avenue, thousands of African Americans leaned out their windows and hung from fire escapes to see the courageous woman who was fighting so hard to end discrimination.

In retrospect, Baker's tour of the United States was a remarkable example of how one person could change the thinking of many in a practical, nonviolent way. Her direct manner of speaking impressed people, and by late 1951, she was seen as a heroine, a woman who spoke simple truths from the heart. But, one evening, the careful plans Baker had made for her career, and the reputation she had built as a leading force against racial discrimination, were shattered when a restaurant refused to serve her a meal.

STORK CLUB SCANDAL

On the night of October 16, Baker performed at the Roxy Theater in New York City. After finishing her show, she and a few friends decided to have dinner at the popular Stork Club on East 53rd Street. Though it was understood that the exclusive club was for whites only, Baker was admitted without comment. She took her seat at a table and ordered a light dinner.

Forty-five minutes later, Baker's friends had been served, but she was still waiting for her meal. Though service at the

Stork Club was often slow, Baker suspected she was being discriminated against. Finally, she called to a waiter and asked him where her steak was. A bit flustered, he told her the restaurant was out of steak. Baker was convinced that the man was lying.

Remaining calm, Baker inquired in a steady voice about the crabmeat cocktail she had ordered. Conversations hushed, meanwhile, and people turned in her direction. The waiter seemed eager to leave. He told Baker that the club no longer served crabmeat cocktails. Then, before she could place a new order, he turned away.

Baker sat at the table for several minutes, thinking the situation over. She was too angry to let the incident pass, and rising, she walked swiftly to the nearest telephone. Walter Winchell, a widely read newspaper columnist, happened to be dining at the Stork Club that evening. As Baker passed, he raised his hand in greeting. (She later claimed he ignored her completely.)

Picking up the receiver, Baker told the operator she wished to speak to Walter White, executive secretary of the NAACP. With that simple request, she set into motion a chain of events that would affect her career for the next 15 years.

By the next morning—October 17, 1951—Josephine Baker had contacted a deputy commissioner of the New York City Police Department and reporters from the *New York Daily News*, in addition to Walter White. To each, she explained what had happened the night before at the Stork Club. The mayor was called, a formal complaint was lodged, and the story hit the papers. Within 72 hours, angry African Americans were picketing in front of New York's most famous night spot.

The protest was successful. But then Baker decided to involve Walter Winchell in the incident.

In 1951, Winchell was the most influential newspaper columnist and radio broadcaster in the United States. More than any other person in the media, he had the power to make or break the careers of actors, politicians, and businessmen. The fashionable Stork Club was Winchell's throne room, and it was there, from table 50, that he usually wrote his column for the *New York Daily Mirror*. His power was both respected and feared, and those who crossed him were usually sorry.

Baker knew of his power, but she believed strongly that the columnist, who had spoken out against discrimination in the past, must be challenged for his failure to help her when she needed him. She accused Winchell of cowardice for refusing to join in her criticism of the Stork Club and for not supporting her in her accusations of what had happened that night.

The columnist was furious. At first, he denied having been at the Stork Club. Then, rethinking his position, he told his radio listeners he was deeply sorry that Baker had been discriminated against. He added, however, that he was "appalled" that she was trying to associate him with the incident.

Many people found themselves taking sides. Prizefighter Sugar Ray Robinson publicly came to Winchell's defense, remembering the times the broadcaster had supported minority rights. The American Newspaper Guild, the NAACP, and Actors' Equity all took Baker's side, as did columnist Ed Sullivan, who said on the radio, "I despise Walter Winchell for what he has done to Josephine Baker." Moments later, Sullivan shocked listeners by calling Winchell a "small-time Hitler."

That comment went too far, and Winchell exploded. In the past, he had publicly admired Baker as an entertainer and civil rights spokeswoman, but that was before his own reputation had been smeared. He fought back, using his column and radio program to accuse "Josa-phoney Baker" of being not only anti-Semitic but "anti-Negro." The charges were ridiculous, of course, but Winchell had a large and loyal following, and many Americans believed whatever he said. Baker's cause was further weakened by the fact that she had become a French citizen.

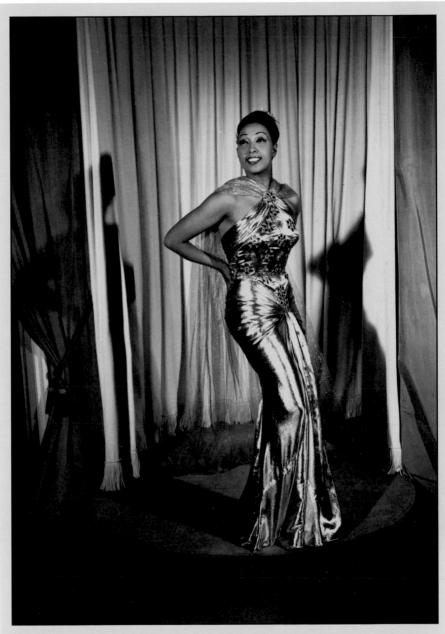

Josephine Baker modeled a gown created by Parisian couturier Pierre Balmain during her U.S. tour in 1951. An incident at the famed Stork Club in New York, where she was refused service, and the resulting fall-out, marred her American tour.

Winchell's criticism of Baker included a suggestion that she was sympathetic to the Communist Party and that some of the African Americans who picketed the Stork Club were also Communists. These were very serious charges, coming at a time when fear of Communism was at a fever pitch in America. Winchell topped off his accusations by insisting that Baker had spent her war years "making oodles of dough in Paris, wining and dining the Nazis and Mussolini's bigwig generals."

The attack was thoroughly unprofessional and hurt not only Baker but Winchell himself. Angry letters began to pour into his New York City office, accusing him of being a coward and a bigot. Newspapers and magazines nationwide began to criticize him. The story even reached France, where the Parisian papers referred to it as *l'Affair du Stork*.

The person who was most hurt, however, was Baker. As the weeks passed, she watched helplessly as concert engagements were canceled one by one. Threatening letters began to arrive at her hotel. A film contract she had just signed was suddenly nullified. Plans to write her life story for an American publisher were dropped. Even African Americans kept their distance, quietly changing tables if Baker sat next to them in a restaurant. Few people, it seemed, wanted to be associated with someone Walter Winchell called a Communist.

The American tour, which had been such a success, turned sour, and Baker felt deeply disappointed. She continued to travel around the country, promoting civil rights whenever she could, but America no longer wanted to hear what she had to say. At last, Baker realized she was fighting a losing battle, and in the summer of 1952 she returned to her chateau in the Dordogne Valley.

There, at last, she found some peace. Construction was progressing smoothly. A restaurant and souvenir shop had opened, gas pumps had been installed, and small huts were built for weekend guests. Riding around the estate in a pony cart, Baker was delighted with the improvements.

Even at this early stage, however, the financial stability of Les Milandes depended entirely on Baker's touring. To help pay the bills, she traveled to Argentina in September for a concert engagement in Buenos Aires. There, her American problems continued.

FBI File on Josephine Baker

Following Josephine Baker's allegations of discrimination at the Stork Club in New York City, the FBI decided to investigate her supposed links to Communism. Within her file were letters Walter Winchell had received and forwarded to the FBI, asking that they be investigated. The letters included this one, which can be found via http://foia.fbi.gov/room.htm:

Dear W.W. (Walter Winchell):

Just read your column on J.B. (Josephine Baker) in today's Daily Mirror, in your last paragraph Mr. Rayburn gives a summation of J.B.'s attitude in the year 1935. In 1936 I visited Leningrad from Helsinki, Finland on a 3 day visit. The month was June "I think"? Anyhow the correct dates on, still on, the U.S.S.R. visa issued in Helsinki on my old passport, a British passport, I'm a Scotchman. Well I wandered into the Russian bar at the hotel one night of the 3 I was there & who was the "Big Shot" of the evening, surrounded by Red Commisars & French Reds, & actually singing & drinking with them to her heart's content, but J.B. The only colored person there. She came to the U.S.S.R. with a large group of French Reds, who in 1936 were being rewarded by the Politbureau for their work in the French Elections that year by a free trip to the U.S.S.R. "as guests of the Soviet Union." If you with your connections "check up" you will probably find J.B. is just a highly colored copy & a poor one at that, of Mati Hari. But still doing her stuff for Uncle Joe. The Reds wined & dined her no end & were laughing up their sleeves at her, as they have no Negroes in the U.S.S.R. she was just a novelty, & a good stooge. Looks to me she is still following the line everywhere she goes.

Sorry she implicated you Walter, but that might have been one of her assignments? You know how the Reds "love you."

Sincerely,
[name blacked out in file]

MISTAKES IN ARGENTINA

In 1952, Juan Perón was the dictator of Argentina. His wife, the beloved Evita, died of cancer that July, and when Baker arrived, the country was still in mourning. Plans were under way to erect an enormous monument to the memory of Evita, and workers were being asked to contribute their wages to pay for its construction.

Like Baker, Evita Perón was a controversial woman who had risen from a childhood of poverty to a position of great wealth and influence. In 1952, the 33-year-old Evita was at the height of her popularity. Two million bereaved Argentines lined the streets of Buenos Aires as her glass-covered coffin passed by.

Baker had been in Argentina only a short time before Juan Perón contacted her. He was deeply grieved by the death of his wife. Evita had been his inspiration, his power—her energy had largely been responsible for his success. Without her, Perón felt lonely and weak. He needed a strong, self-made woman to continue his wife's work, someone who could lead the masses. Someone with a name. Someone like Baker.

Flattered by Perón's compliments, and sincerely believing he was a good and honest leader, Baker agreed to assume some of Evita's duties. At a memorial rally, speaking before a large crowd of working-class people, Baker delivered a stirring speech in which she praised Argentina for being an "enlightened democracy," which it certainly was not. Perón's Argentina was a Fascist state, one that severely limited the rights of its citizens. No one could speak out against Perón without fear of imprisonment.

Baker was very naive, however, when it came to understanding political situations. She rarely troubled herself with learning the facts; almost always, she listened to her heart and acted accordingly. This combination of ignorance and innocence further poisoned her relations with the United States.

Over the next several months, Baker consistently spoke out against America, calling it a "barbarous land living in a false,

Nazi-style democracy." Nor did she have any faith in the newly elected president, Dwight D. Eisenhower. "Black people will suffer as they have never suffered," she said. "May God have pity on them."

Señora Baker, as she was called, stayed in Argentina for six months, visiting hospitals, meeting with the press, and recommending to the government which charities should receive support. As she understood it, her job was essentially one of goodwill. In reality, it was a mask designed to hide the injustices of Perón's regime.

Gradually, though, even Baker began to see the situation for what it was. She noticed, for instance, that many Argentines were living in terrible poverty, that hospital care was frequently inadequate, and that mentally disturbed patients were treated like animals in the asylums. Evita Perón, she learned, had nearly bankrupted the nation with her extravagant tastes for clothing and jewelry. Baker heard persistent rumors that the army was dissatisfied, that corruption existed at every level of the government, that Juan Perón's secret police used brutal methods to deal with political enemies.

Finally, in the spring of 1953, Baker realized that she no longer wanted to represent Juan Perón. Confused and distressed, she returned to France, to the familiar surroundings of Les Milandes. There, she felt compelled to do some serious thinking about her life. Her efforts to end discrimination had been largely unsuccessful, and at the age of 47, she wondered what she would accomplish in the years ahead.

9

The Rainbow Tribe

Ever since the end of the war, a dream had slowly been developing in the back of Josephine Baker's mind. Now, with Jo Bouillon's help, she wanted to see it come true. It would bring together all of her ideas about equality and what she called the "brotherhood of man."

As Baker saw it, there was no valid reason why all the races could not live together in peace—the world only needed to be shown how. Les Milandes, with its eating and sleeping facilities, large vegetable gardens, church, cemetery, and nearby river, had already become something of a small city. In her mind's eye, Baker could easily see it as a global village. (She had installed, in fairy-tale fashion, a tiny post office near the chateau; its stamps were not recognized by the French postal service, but the post office made Baker feel as if she were living in her own private kingdom.)

In this quiet spot, removed from the world's prejudices, Baker hoped to adopt many children of different nationalities. By raising them in an atmosphere of love and equality, she would show the world that racial harmony was not only possible but absolutely vital.

As usual, Baker's dream was a costly one, but she believed in it so passionately that she refused to let anything stand in her way. By 1953, she and Bouillon had turned Les Milandes into a lovely resort, with a plush hotel, a swimming pool, a pleasure garden, paddle-boats, a theater, an amusement park, and a special museum devoted to the highlights of Baker's life. It was an ideal environment in which to raise children.

In early 1954, after filling several rooms with baby furniture, Baker set off for Tokyo, Japan. There, she adopted two baby boys, the first members of what would come to be known as the Rainbow Tribe: Akio, who was Korean, and Janot, who was Japanese.

As a representative of the International League Against Racism and Anti-Semitism, Baker also gave several lectures in Osaka and Tokyo. With the aid of an interpreter, she stressed the importance of world peace.

Baker enjoyed public speaking and, later that year, she traveled to Scandinavia to give more lectures. While in Helsinki, she adopted a two-year-old Finn named Jari, a chubby little boy who took great delight in making it as difficult as possible for Baker to pick him up.

Then, in 1955, it was off to Central and South America. One evening in Bogotá, a poor Colombian woman appeared in the lobby of Baker's hotel, carrying a baby wrapped in a dirty shawl. She held the bundle out to Baker, explaining that he was her eighth child and that she could not afford to raise him. Within 24 hours, adoption arrangements were made, and little Luis joined the Rainbow Tribe.

At this point, Bouillon became concerned. Financially, he was a cautious, practical man, and he could see that the expenses were starting to get out of hand. He tried to discuss the matter with his wife, but Baker's answer was firm. As long as they could afford governesses, she saw no reason to delay the adoptions. Besides, she felt it was her God-given responsibility to help as many children as she could.

It was not long before the Bouillons had taken in three more infants: Marianne and Jean-Claude, who were French, and Brahim, who was Arab. The growing Tribe attracted a great deal of attention from the press and the public. More than 300,000 tourists flocked to Les Milandes each summer to see this unconventional experiment in humanity. Still, there never seemed to be quite enough money.

In her attempt to mix children of different nationalities and religions, Baker traveled to Israel, where she tried, unsuccessfully, to adopt a Jewish boy. Israel, a new country, was trying to develop its population, and Baker was unable to persuade the government to release an Israeli youngster.

She refused to give up, however, and simply adopted a Jewish child through an organization based in Paris. The boy's name was Moses (Moïse), and Baker would make an effort to provide him with a proper Jewish education. By the time the boy's lessons began, however, little Moses was more interested in sitting by the swimming pool than in studying Hebrew texts. When Baker did nothing to encourage her son's studies, Moses's tutor quit in frustration.

Unfortunately, he was not the first, or last, teacher to walk out the gates of Les Milandes in anger. From the very beginning, Baker stubbornly refused to discipline her children. As an entertainer, she was able to spend only a limited amount of time with the family. It was vital, therefore, that every moment with the children be as enjoyable as possible. Sharp words and spankings had no place at Les Milandes.

Another, more serious, problem was Baker's marriage. Because she was on tour so often, Baker felt removed from the day-to-day problems at the chateau. She never had to deal with

Josephine Baker and Jo Bouillon kiss one of their adopted children, Akio, in the newly opened nightclub at their home, Les Milandes. The other children with them in this photograph from 1956 were (from left) Luis, Jean-Claude, Janot, Jari, and Moses. Baker would eventually adopt 12 children of different races and nationalities.

the food shopping or the cleaning of the pool or the checking-in of guests or any of the thousand little details that kept the resort running smoothly. Leaky faucets were simply not her concern, and over a period of time, she began to regard her husband as little more than the caretaker at Les Milandes. During her brief visits home, she was jealous that he knew the children better than she did, and his constant lectures about money annoyed her.

Baker realized that her marriage was in trouble, but she did not know how to save it. More than once, she promised to retire, but the costs associated with running the chateau and raising eight children were extraordinary. By 1957, the

Bouillons were more than 83 million francs in debt. Even if Baker had wanted to quit the stage, it would have been financially impossible.

For Bouillon, the breaking point came in early 1957, when Baker brought home a little boy named Koffi, an orphan from the Ivory Coast in Africa. Repeatedly, Bouillon tried to explain to Baker the tremendous financial strain she was putting on the family, but Baker refused to listen. As far as she was concerned, she was working for the good of humankind. This lofty, unrealistic approach led to a series of arguments that eventually shattered the marriage. One afternoon, Baker went so far as to gather the servants in the hallway, hysterically demanding that they choose between her and her husband. "If you're on his side, stand over there," she insisted, pointing to the other side of the room.

A separation was clearly in order, and in late 1957, Bouillon packed his belongings and moved to Paris, where he resumed his career as an orchestra conductor. He and Baker delayed getting a divorce, though. At heart, neither was eager to see the marriage end, especially with nine children involved.

FINANCING A FAMILY

With difficulty, Baker took over the management of Les Milandes. Ignoring the 83 million francs she owed, she ordered further construction, never even asking about the cost. Finances confused and bored her, and she stayed as far away from them as possible.

Instead, Baker devoted her energy to the Rainbow Tribe, taking the children on tour whenever it could be arranged. She particularly enjoyed introducing them to their native lands. In 1958, for instance, little Jari was able to visit Finland, where Baker was giving a concert in Helsinki. In no time, traveling became a happy way of life for the nine youngsters.

In the spring of that year, Jo Bouillon returned to Les Milandes, determined to rescue his marriage. The reconciliation

To raise the money needed for her large family, Josephine Baker often had to go on tour. Here, she was performing in her show *Paris, mes Amours* at the Olympia Theater in Paris in 1957.

was bumpy. For one, Baker refused to curb her spending. On every tour, she bought dozens of dresses, scarves, blouses, and hats. She also purchased presents for the children, who called her, appropriately, Mama Cadeau (Mother Gift). Ignoring the entertainment budget, she brought in expensive orchestras and ballet troupes, and foolishly began to buy up all the land around Les Milandes.

Then, to her husband's considerable shock, she adopted two more infants, bringing the Rainbow Tribe to 11. The first child, Mara, was a malnourished Venezuelan Indian; the second, Noël, had been abandoned on the streets of Paris. Baker was convinced that God had saved the infants for a reason and, though she knew the adoptions would cause further financial hardship, she could never turn her back on a child in need.

Bouillon realized then that their differences were irreconcilable. Shortly after Noël's adoption, he packed and moved to a small apartment in Paris. The marriage, which had lasted nearly 13 years, was over.

Left on her own, Baker embarked on the most turbulent and stressful period of her life. Lacking Bouillon's business sense, she allowed the debts at the world village to grow astronomically. One by one, merchants began to cut off the steady stream of supplies to Les Milandes. Most of these local tradespeople wanted to see Baker succeed, but they could not live on promises and IOUs. There was a time when Baker was so popular she could have walked into nearly any store in Paris, done her shopping, and never have been charged for her purchases. Now, she could not buy a pound of butter without paying cash on the spot.

The only practical solution was for Baker to declare bankruptcy, which she would not do. In her heart, she believed that God was watching out for her.

In January 1961, it looked as if Baker's patience would finally be rewarded. One afternoon, she was contacted by a European director, Ernst Marischka, who hoped to make a film about the Rainbow Tribe. He was certain the project would be a success, and the money that Baker would receive would be more than enough to save Les Milandes. With one simple signature, all her financial troubles would be solved.

Baker thought the matter over carefully and, finally, after a long, sleepless night, she said no. A movie, she feared, would exploit the children and somehow cheapen what she was try-ing to do. Above all, she wanted her youngsters to be able to go out into the world and teach other people the racial tolerance they had learned at Les Milandes. She was afraid that a film might change their outlook and their values. She could not take that chance.

The decision was extremely difficult for Baker. Little by little, she could see that Les Milandes was slipping away, and the thought agonized her. A few weeks after she rejected the film offer, she sat down and tried to write out her feelings.

"I don't know how or where I'm going," she began. "How will I manage? I have only a few thousand francs left. Everything's going wrong." Then, in a moment of remarkable insight, Baker added, "But I also realize *how difficult it must be to live with people like me.*"

And yet, despite all her troubles and worries, there were still many happy days at Les Milandes. Life with Josephine Baker was always an adventure, a roller-coaster ride full of unexpected surprises. That summer, for instance, she participated in one of the proudest ceremonies of her life, when the French Republic named her a Chevalier of the Legion of Honor. The award was given not only in recognition of her wartime work but also for her peacetime effort to educate the world about the injustice of discrimination.

The impressive ceremony took place in August 1961 at Les Milandes and was attended by representatives from six nations, including the United States. Baker was deeply moved by the honor. Speaking to the crowd, she commended France as "the only place in the world where I can quietly and surely realize my dream." Afterward, as photographers rushed forward, the Rainbow Tribe hugged Baker around the knees and presented her with bouquets of freshly picked flowers.

That fall, Bosley Crowther, the film critic for *The New York Times*, expressed a desire to write a book about Baker's life. He was not the first person to suggest the idea, nor would he be the last. (As early as the 1930s, there had been talk of turning Baker's life into a play.) Sadly, Crowther's book was never written. In fact, none of the creative projects inspired by La Bakaire ever materialized during her lifetime.

The next few years were agonizing for Baker. She toured constantly, but her income quickly evaporated as a result of poor business decisions and outrageous spending habits. (She found it necessary, for instance, to liven up the barnyard by spelling out the cows' names in electric lights.) By 1963, Les Milandes was nearly $400,000 in debt. The situation was critical, and Baker was forced to sell her jewelry collection to pay the bills.

Unwisely, Baker decided to adopt another child: Stellina, the twelfth and final member of the Rainbow Tribe. Stellina was a beautiful but delicate Moroccan baby born in France. Jo Bouillon, who was preparing to move to Buenos Aires, agreed to sign the adoption papers.

As a social experiment, the Rainbow Tribe never achieved great importance. When Baker started her family in 1954, she had hoped to prove to the world that all races could live together harmoniously. If she had limited the adoptions to a reasonable number—say, five or six—the village would almost certainly have flourished. Instead, she adopted twice that many children, while continuing to make expensive renovations to her home. The social value of Baker's experiment was largely ignored by the press, which focused instead on her financial problems. In an age when the issue of civil rights was taking on new importance, it must have sickened Baker to realize that the Rainbow Tribe was no longer newsworthy.

10

Great Dreams

Josephine Baker's Rainbow Tribe represented a small step in the fight for equality, but younger activists were now leading the civil rights movement. In the United States, definite changes were taking place. African Americans were demanding equal justice under the law; segregation was a highly controversial issue; and a 34-year-old Baptist minister named Martin Luther King, Jr., was at the forefront of the civil rights movement. In August 1963, he and other black leaders were planning a march in the nation's capital to highlight the importance of black equality.

Baker was determined to participate, but to her shock, the U.S. Immigration and Naturalization Service stood in her way. Her anti-American statements and Walter Winchell's insistence that she was a Communist had not been forgotten. Fortunately, the U.S. attorney general, Robert Kennedy, decided to help her. He persuaded his brother, President

John F. Kennedy, to launch an investigation into Baker's political background.

After a thorough inquiry, the Kennedys decided that Baker was not a Communist—or anything else, for that matter. Her beliefs concerning brotherhood were simply too naive to make her an effective member of any political organization. It was obvious, at least to the Kennedys, that she presented no threat to the American government, and instructions were sent to the Immigration and Naturalization Service to admit Baker without delay.

The March on Washington for Jobs and Freedom took place on August 28, 1963, and was, at the time, the largest civil rights gathering in American history. With 250,000 other equal rights supporters, Baker marched to the Lincoln Memorial, where a large platform had been erected for a rally. It was a hot, sunny day, and the rally, which began at 1:00 P.M., was broadcast on live television. Dr. King introduced a variety of speakers, then invited Baker to say a few words. By this time, the heat was intense and the crowd was beginning to grow restless. Baker, wearing her wartime uniform, walked quietly to the microphone and stared out at the sea of people before her. "I am so happy to be here," she said, her voice choked with emotion.

For the next few minutes, Baker spoke of her difficult childhood in St. Louis, the equality she had known in France, and the equality that would surely come to the United States. She filled her listeners with hope and dignity and a keen sense of brotherhood. When she finished her speech and turned away from the microphone, the applause was deafening. People stomped their feet and broke into joyous song. Many had never heard of Josephine Baker before, but her simple words won them over.

Taking her seat, Baker watched as Martin Luther King, the final speaker of the day, stepped to the microphone. With great conviction, he, too, mesmerized the crowd with a speech that would be remembered as the greatest of his career. "I have a dream," he told his listeners, "that one day this nation will rise up and live out the true meaning of its creed: We hold these truths to be self-evident, that all men are created equal."

The effect of the March on Washington could be felt all over the country. The following year, King was awarded the Nobel Peace Prize, and the U.S. Congress passed the Civil Rights Act of 1964, outlawing most forms of racial discrimination. Progress was finally being made.

As Baker boarded the plane to return to France, she was filled with a renewed sense of determination. Now, it seemed more important than ever to save Les Milandes. The problems that awaited her at home, however, were considerable. Not only were the debts enormous, but the situation with the servants was becoming unmanageable. Because Baker could not afford to pay salaries promptly, employees were coming and going at regular intervals. Governesses were almost impossible to keep—they found Baker unpredictable and bossy, and they resented being told how to care for the children. In their bitterness, some employees began to steal.

The popularity of Les Milandes was also steadily declining. Interest in the world village had faded; people preferred to see Baker in Paris, descending the glamorous staircase of the Olympia Theater. The deterioration of the chateau tormented her terribly. At night, she could not sleep, racked with worry, trying to figure out some way to save the estate. At age 57, she knew she could not rely on touring much longer. Somehow, Les Milandes had to become self-sufficient.

Gradually, Baker became convinced that it would be most practical to establish a large school on the property. She even came up with a lofty name for the institution: the International Brotherhood College. The school, which she hoped would attract 500 young adults, would offer a broad variety of courses. The overall emphasis would be on human relations.

Prejudice, Baker believed, was the result of ignorance and distrust. Real freedom, then, could only come about through education. People had to learn about equality before they could practice it. Baker saw her school as revolutionary, one that would attract professors and speakers from all over the world. With spacious dormitories and communal eating halls, it would be similar to her global village, only on a larger scale.

The cost to build and maintain the college would be staggering, but Baker refused to give up on the idea. For the next several years, she toured frequently and, in one newspaper interview after another, she explained her financial situation to the public. She was delighted when envelopes containing money began to arrive at Les Milandes. Usually, the envelopes held only small amounts—$5 or $10—but they were a step in the right direction.

Influential friends and celebrities also did what they could to help. Film actress Brigitte Bardot appeared on a French television program that raised nearly $25,000 for Les Milandes. King Hassan II of Morocco, Empress Farah Diba of Iran, and Yvonne de Gaulle (wife of the president of France), all

IN HER OWN WORDS...

At the March on Washington, Josephine Baker was deeply moved by the sight of hundreds of thousands of participants, black and white. According to *Jazz Cleopatra: Josephine Baker in Her Time* by Phyllis Rose, Baker told the crowd:

> You are on the eve of a complete victory. You can't go wrong. The world is behind you. Salt and pepper. Just what it should be.

sent money. A Swiss bank lent Baker a substantial amount. All this help came just in time: the electricity and water at Les Milandes had been shut off for lack of payment, and Baker's creditors had gone to court to have her possessions sold at auction.

The hard work and constant worry took their toll. On July 25, 1964, Baker suffered a heart attack and was rushed to the hospital. Even then, she could not stop. She had to calculate how much the hospital bill would be and how much work would be required to cover the loss. On October 24, she suffered a second heart attack.

Plans for the university continued, meanwhile, and in early 1965 Baker contacted an Italian architect, Bruno Fedrigolli, who began to draw designs for the classrooms, dormitories, and offices that would surround the ancient chateau. Wherever she went, Baker spoke about the college and how it would promote goodwill and understanding among people of all races.

"We must change the system of education and instruction," she wrote. "Unfortunately, history has shown us that brotherhood must be learned, when it should be natural."

To Baker's surprise, the Cuban dictator Fidel Castro took an interest in her dream. In July 1966, her family was invited to spend a month's vacation in one of Castro's villas. The Cuban holiday was delightful, and each child received a personal gift from "Uncle Fidel" before leaving the island. Castro also promised he would send a special gift to Les Milandes. Naturally, Baker assumed it would be money, enough to save the chateau and start the college.

She was wrong. Castro's gift was not a check but a large box of Cuban fruit.

King Hassan's generosity proved to be more practical. The Moroccan ruler offered Baker a large piece of land in Marrakech, where she could rebuild her life and begin construction of the International Brotherhood College. The offer was extremely tempting, but in her heart Baker knew she could not turn her back on Les Milandes. Furthermore, she felt it was vital that the college be built in France, which she considered a true democracy.

The decision was a brave one, especially because the creditors were constantly at Baker's side, pressuring her, nagging her. A list had already been drawn up of her household possessions, and Baker knew that any day they might be sold to the highest bidder. Somehow, she managed to raise enough money to avoid each auction, but it was always a desperate race against time.

HOMELESS

By 1968, not only was Baker's dream crumbling, so was Les Milandes. She could no longer afford to pay gardeners, and weeds began to sprout between the paving stones. Water leaked through the roof, staining the expensive Oriental rugs. The paddle-boats were faded, their paint peeling off into the water. In February, Baker narrowly avoided another attempt to auction off the chateau. Her debts at this point totaled a staggering 150 million francs.

When Les Milandes finally collapsed, it happened exactly as Baker feared. The creditors could wait no longer, and an auction was scheduled for the spring of 1968.

On May 3, the day of the auction, Baker happened to be on tour in Scandinavia. Sitting in her hotel room in Göteborg, Sweden, she nervously watched the clock, waiting for someone to phone her with the bad news. As the minutes ticked by, she tried to jot down her thoughts. "I'm sitting here sick at heart," she wrote. "Will Les Milandes be put up for sale at two o'clock or not? ... I'm determined to fight this through.... The forty-five minutes are up now. The auction has begun."

Three hours later, the phone call came. "*I'm afraid I've got very bad news,*" Baker wrote. "*At four o'clock Les Milandes was sold for 125 million francs.*"

Her luck had finally run out.

By June, Baker's tour had ended. She was out of work and would soon be homeless. How could she continue to raise 12 children under those circumstances? Once again, the constant worry took its toll, and on July 4, Baker suffered a minor stroke.

Fortunately, her recovery was swift. Baker was determined to beat her troubles no matter what it took. No sooner had she recovered, however, than Akio, her eldest child, had to be rushed to the hospital for an emergency appendectomy. One misfortune seemed to follow another.

A formal notice was sent to Les Milandes to inform Baker that she and the children had to be off the property by October 7. The eviction was delayed, however, and the family spent the last remaining months living together in one room, desperately trying to figure out some way to buy back the property. The situation was sad and hopeless.

The following January, Baker watched helplessly as the furniture was auctioned off, piece by piece. Everything was sold, from the dining room chairs to the cat's food dish. A treasured letter from President Charles de Gaulle sold for only one franc.

When it came time to leave, the children walked along the banks of the Dordogne, tearfully hugging the trees good-bye. The Rainbow Tribe was then sent to live with a friend in Paris, while Baker stayed behind to fight for their legal rights. She was firmly convinced that she had been swindled, that the property was legally still hers. When it became obvious that the law was no longer on her side, she crawled through a window and barricaded herself in the kitchen. The new owner of Les Milandes had no patience for this sort of behavior. One morning, he sent over a group of neighborhood toughs to force her out.

The scene that followed was appalling. As the men hauled Baker through the kitchen, she grabbed onto the stove so tightly her fingers had to be pried off. Next, they kicked the back door open and roughly pushed her out, onto the back stoop. She sat there in the rain, like a crumpled rag doll, for the next seven hours. Finally, an ambulance arrived and took her to a nearby hospital, where she was admitted for nervous exhaustion.

After many desperate years, the story of Les Milandes was over. Baker had been beaten.

FRESH START

A few weeks later, Baker returned to Paris, collected the children, and moved to a small, rented apartment on the avenue MacMahon. The sale of the chateau had done little to ease Baker's financial troubles. There were still many bills to pay and many mouths to feed. At one time, in 1930, Baker had been the wealthiest black woman in the world. Now, she was living in a two-room apartment with 12 children and two dogs. If there was ever a time in her life when she needed help, it was now.

One can easily imagine Baker's surprise, then, when Princess Grace of Monaco offered to lend a hand. In 1969, the princess was one of the most respected women in the world. A beautiful, award-winning actress, she had retired from her film career in 1956 to marry Prince Rainier of Monaco. Their lavish wedding was regarded around the world as a fairy tale come true. By coincidence, Princess Grace had been dining at the Stork Club that evening in 1951 when Baker was denied service. The incident deeply upset her, and she had admired Baker's courage in standing up for her civil rights. Now, reading of Les Milandes's auction, Princess Grace invited Baker to perform at a special benefit that August for the Monaco Red Cross.

Though she would not be paid for her appearance, Baker accepted the invitation. Her performance that summer night created a sensation. For a full 90 minutes, she treated the audience to an unforgettable evening of passionate singing and nimble dancing. When she broke into her famous Charleston, it seemed impossible that this was the same Josephine Baker who, only months earlier, had sat weeping in the rain on her

A distraught Josephine Baker, above, sat on the steps of Les Milandes for seven hours after being forcibly evicted from the chateau in 1969. Les Milandes was auctioned off the year before to pay the debts that Baker incurred while taking care of her large family.

back stoop. The transformation was breathtaking. At the end of the show, the crowd threw roses onto the stage while whistling and shouting its approval.

The revue played for an entire week, and word of Baker's triumph quickly spread throughout Europe. To her delight, invitations and contracts began to arrive at her hotel. Originally, she had planned to return to Paris at the end of August, but she decided to make her permanent home near the tiny principality of Monaco. With Princess Grace's approval, the Red Cross gave Baker $20,000 as a down payment for a house in nearby Roquebrune, about three miles from Monte Carlo. The four-bedroom villa, which she named Maryvonne, clung dramatically to the rocks above the sea.

The Baker clan quickly settled into its new life. When Baker was not on tour, she delighted in roaming the picturesque streets, a shopping basket on one arm, several of the children tagging along behind her. In a way, it was the fairytale environment she had tried so hard to create for herself at Les Milandes.

Little Stellina, the youngest of the Rainbow Tribe, was sent to a local elementary school, where she attended class with Princess Stephanie, Princess Grace's youngest daughter. The other Baker children were growing older and more independent, and to their mother's distress, they no longer needed her as much. Gradually, they had come to resent her continual absences and now remained emotionally distant whenever she returned home from a tour. It was difficult for them to appreciate their mother's hard work, and their indifference hurt her badly. The children were very loyal to one another, however, and Baker was gratified that, in at least one way, her Rainbow experiment had been a success.

The early 1970s were extremely busy for Baker. She continued to take the Rainbow Tribe on tour, making sure each child was introduced to his or her native country. Also during this period, the dream of the International Brotherhood College was revived. Marshal Tito, the president of Yugoslavia, had followed the ups and downs of Baker's life, and he knew how much the college meant to her. In the spirit of generosity, he offered her an island off the coast of Yugoslavia, where she could live with her family and build her university. He even promised her that the government would install electricity and phone lines, bring in water, and build roads.

Baker was tempted to accept the offer. Gradually, however, she realized that, even with Yugoslavian help, the International Brotherhood College would be vastly expensive. She considered selling the villa in Monaco, until she was reminded that the house had not yet been paid for; she could not sell what she did not own. The Brotherhood College was never built—although, after her initial disappointment, Baker realized it was probably for the best. It would almost certainly have ruined her financially, and she was too old to repeat the tragedy of Les Milandes.

Instead, Baker resumed her international tours. Nearly every concert now was a success, and she felt highly optimistic about the future. In a happy state of mind, she decided to return to the United States in 1973 to perform at New York City's prestigious Carnegie Hall. Her old adversary, Walter Winchell, had died the previous year, and her friends felt certain that her return to the States would be a success.

RETURN OF A LEGEND

Baker flew to New York in June 1973, just before her sixty-seventh birthday. Flyers were being distributed throughout the city. BLACK LEGEND RETURNS, they announced in large letters. The response was enthusiastic, and when Baker walked onstage on opening night, the audience rose to its feet and gave her the warmest, most sincere ovation she had ever received in the United States. Wild applause echoed through the hall, drowning out the orchestra. Tears filled Baker's eyes before the concert had even begun.

"I didn't think that I would be so well-received," she said, deeply moved by the ovation.

Baker's singing voice was no longer the sweet instrument it had once been. That night, in fact, it was particularly hoarse, because of the summer humidity. The audience members did not care. They seemed perfectly happy just to be in the presence of the legendary Josephine Baker. As she sang and danced, a single red rose was passed from hand to hand, a delicate symbol of unity and love.

The highlight of the show was a medley of memories from Baker's long and exciting career. She took the audience back to 1925, when she first arrived in Paris for *La Revue Nègre*. There were only a few black people in the city at that time, she explained, and her dark skin had enchanted the Parisians. "They said, 'Isn't it beautiful to be kissed by the sun in that way?'"

At the end of the show, Baker referred to her long struggle against racial discrimination. "Friends and family," she said, "I did take the blows [of life], but I took them with my chin up, in dignity, because I so profoundly love and respect humanity."

The applause that evening was shattering, and the reviews the next day were among the finest of her career. Thrilled with her success, Baker decided to tour the country that fall. In the meantime, however, she flew to Copenhagen for a concert engagement, taking Brahim, Koffi, Noël, and Mara with her.

One afternoon, the four boys sat waiting in the hotel room for Baker to return. After several hours, they decided to call the hospital, and they received bad news: She had suffered a heart attack and a stroke. The boys immediately rushed to her bedside, but Baker, barely conscious, did not recognize them. There was nothing the children could do, so they left the hospital and went to the nearest church, where they prayed for their mother's recovery.

Fortunately, Baker was back on her feet within a short time. It gradually became apparent, however, that the stroke had affected her mind, taking away its former sharpness. Every now and then, she forgot the lyrics to her songs. She confused names and dates. She worried that the public would notice, so she openly apologized for her mistakes. "I'm too old to play Josephine Baker," she told her friends.

By Christmas, her memory had become so poor that it was almost embarrassing to watch her at times, and this was

Josephine Baker performed at a Franco-American gala on November 27, 1973, at the Palace of Versailles. That same year, Baker had a successful engagement at Carnegie Hall in New York City.

mentioned in most newspaper reviews. In her heart, Baker knew it would be best to retire quietly, but financially that was impossible. The expenses at the villa were a constant burden. To save money, she began to eat cheap meals and buy budget clothing for the children. Occasionally, she even asked strangers for money. She was determined to stretch every dollar as far as it could go.

In 1974, the Monaco Red Cross once again invited Baker to perform at its annual fund-raising benefit. This time, the revue not only starred Josephine Baker, it was about her. André Levasseur, the stage designer, wanted the new show to be something special, and *Josephine's Story* seemed the perfect answer. The success or failure of the autobiographical revue would depend largely on Baker's memory, and she accepted the challenge with gusto. As rehearsals got under way, she made it clear that she hoped to take the show to Paris the following spring.

A skillful combination of drama and music, *Josephine's Story* was a hit when it opened in early August. The star's appearance at the beginning of the show was unforgettable: Drawn onstage in a carriage, she stepped out to reveal herself wrapped in 225 yards of fine silk. The effect was stunning, and for the next hour, Baker pulled out all the stops, throwing herself into every song and every dance. The reviews the next morning were glowing. A MILESTONE IN THE HISTORY OF MUSIC HALL, one headline trumpeted.

Sadly, however, the producers could not persuade a single theater in Paris to book *Josephine's Story*. The Parisian managers complained that she was a has-been, and to her disappointment, Baker was forced to go on the road again, touring London, Stockholm, Tel Aviv, Johannesburg, and Cape Town. André Levasseur, meanwhile, did his best to get the Parisian managers to rethink their decisions. The show, he told them, could be a sensation if they would only give it a chance.

Finally, after months of meetings and discussions, the Bobino Theater in Paris agreed to stage the revue. Baker was overjoyed and, at the same time, somewhat apprehensive. She sensed that this was her last chance to succeed in Paris; consequently, she pushed herself harder than she ever had before. The rehearsals frequently ran past midnight, but she never complained and was usually the first to arrive at the theater the next morning.

As opening night approached, word spread through Paris that something wonderful was happening at the Bobino. Crowds gathered at the front door, straining to hear the music inside. Onstage, La Bakaire was doing the Charleston, the same dance with which she had conquered Paris 50 years earlier. The revue, which had been retitled *Josephine*, was more than two hours long, and the star had to memorize more than 30 musical numbers. It would have been an extraordinary challenge for the youngest of performers. For a 68-year-old woman with a failing memory and other health problems, it was nothing short of a miracle.

Several performances were given for the public before the official opening. Each evening, Baker studied the crowd's reaction. She continually tightened the pace, rearranged songs, and dropped entire scenes if she felt they were slowing down the action. No detail was too small to be ignored. Baker thought that if the show was a hit, she could take it on the road and, within a year's time, earn enough money to retire finally.

The gala opening on April 8, 1975, was everything Baker hoped it would be. From the moment she appeared onstage, Paris went wild. It was 1925 all over again, and the city welcomed her with open arms.

For the next two hours, Baker held the audience spellbound as she drove across the stage on a motorcycle, danced a furious Charleston, saluted *Shuffle Along*, paraded down the grand staircase in a variety of stunning outfits, and, of course, introduced her favorite animals. She even passed out pieces of sugarcane and, sitting in a dusty jeep in her French Air Force uniform, she reminisced about the war.

It was as if Baker were trying to squeeze an entire lifetime into one evening. She succeeded brilliantly. The older Parisians wept tears of nostalgia. The younger Parisians, who knew nothing of Baker, were amazed. Who was she, they asked, and why had they never seen her before?

By the time the curtain fell, Baker had reconquered the city of her youth. For the next 24 hours, she was the toast of Paris again: Everyone wanted to be near her, to touch her, to get her autograph. The president of France, Valéry Giscard d'Estaing, sent a telegram to congratulate her on her 50-year triumph. London and New York sent word that they wanted to book the show. Tickets at the Bobino, meanwhile, were sold out a month in advance. At last, it looked as if Baker's money troubles were over.

On the morning of Thursday, April 10, Baker slept much later than usual. A friend, Lélia Scotto, who was staying with Baker at the time, could hear light snoring through the bedroom door, so she thought nothing of it. It was not until 5:00 P.M. that Scotto realized something was wrong. A bit frightened, she rapped on the bedroom door, but there was no answer. Peering in, she discovered Baker stretched out motionless on the bed, newspapers strewn about her. She must have been reading the reviews of her show when, at some point earlier that afternoon, she slipped into a coma.

An ambulance was immediately summoned, and Baker was rushed to the Salpêtrière Hospital, where she remained in critical condition for the next 36 hours. Word leaked out, and on Friday the hospital was swamped with newspaper reporters and photographers. Princess Grace was in Paris at the time, and she hurried to her friend's bedside, where she prayed fervently for Baker's recovery.

An urgent telegram was sent to Jo Bouillon in Buenos Aires. JOSEPHINE IN SERIOUS CONDITION, it read. He immediately departed for Paris, but sadly, he arrived a few hours too late. Josephine Baker died at 5:00 A.M. on Saturday, April 12, 1975, at the age of 68. The cause of her death was a cerebral hemorrhage. One friend, however, thought differently: "In my opinion, she died of joy."

The funeral, which was held three days later, was an enormous affair. Even though it was a drizzly afternoon, thousands of people crowded the streets to catch a glimpse of the closed coffin as it passed. Older Parisians, those who remembered Baker well, tossed bouquets of flowers onto the moving hearse. With great pomp, the military fired a 21-gun salute, an honor usually reserved for heads of state.

Inside the Church of the Madeleine, Baker's coffin was draped with the French flag, upon which rested a large cross of red and white roses. Nearby, her war medals were proudly displayed on a satin pillow. Hundreds of candles shimmered warmly as the organist played a selection of Baker's most popular songs, filling the church with rich and extraordinary memories: of triumphs and setbacks, of St. Louis ragtime and the French Resistance, of leopards and monkeys and banana skirts, of dignity and discrimination, and of a noble experiment called the Rainbow Tribe.

It was Josephine Baker's finale—a grand exit to a remarkable life.

THE LEGACY

Josephine Baker's legacy extended over several decades and included critical points in the history of France and the United States. First and foremost, as a dancer she popularized a new, energetic, and passionate style of dance, a raw form of an art that had been carefully staged and choreographed until that point. She exposed European audiences to African-American rhythms and music, and influenced European dancers and choreographers, resulting in a new fusion of style that became extraordinarily popular.

The funeral procession for Josephine Baker passed by the Bobino Theater, where she had just opened her latest show, *Josephine*, to great fanfare a few days before. Baker died of a cerebral hemorrhage on April 12, 1975, but in one friend's opinion, "she died of joy."

She also glamorized a new type of beauty in France. The girl who had once been deemed "too dark and too skinny" for a place in the chorus line became a woman who was admired and imitated. Women tried to darken their skin and style their hair to more closely resemble "the black Venus."

Baker challenged racial barriers throughout her career. Her performances attracted black and white audiences. Entertaining troops during World War II, she ensured that the soldiers attending her shows were not segregated. She became, for a time, one of the wealthiest women in Paris.

Baker's service to France during World War II exemplified her commitment to her adopted country. She joined the Resistance and courageously served as a secret agent, risking her own life and her career.

She continued to challenge discrimination whenever she encountered it. Her public protest after the Stork Club refused to serve her damaged her career, but she demonstrated that famous celebrities were not exempt from prejudice and racial bias. As he only woman speaker at the 1963 March on Washington, she served as a reminder that the struggle for equality had a long history, and that women as well as men had been pioneers in the fight for civil rights.

Baker was a pioneer—in dance, in women's rights, in civil rights. She believed in a world where people of different races could live together, as brothers and sisters, and she tried to make her belief a reality. As she wrote in *Josephine*, her posthumously published memoir, "I've taken my task so much to heart that it's become all I live for. I've had some wonderful moments during my battle. Neither threats nor loss of work can keep me from continuing to fight for my beliefs. Just the opposite. They serve to convince me that I'm in the right."

1906 Born Freda Josephine McDonald on June 3 in St. Louis, Missouri

circa 1919 Marries Willie Wells; leaves St. Louis with the Jones Family Band and the Dixie Steppers

1921 Marries Willie Baker

1922 Joins the cast of *Shuffle Along*

1924 Stars in *The Chocolate Dandies*

1925 Appears at the Plantation Club in New York City; sails for Paris; opens on October 2 in *La Revue Nègre*

1926 Debuts at the Folies Bergère in Paris

1927 Publishes her first book, *Les Mémoires de Joséphine Baker*; makes her first film, *La Sirène des Tropiques*

1928 Begins her first world tour

1934 Stars in Jacques Offenbach's operetta *La Créole*

1936 Appears in *Ziegfeld Follies* in New York City

1937 Marries Jean Lion; becomes a French citizen

1940 Is recruited to work for French military intelligence during World War II

1941 Becomes seriously ill while in Casablanca

1943 Begins tour to entertain Allied troops

1946 Receives the Medal of the Resistance with Rosette from the French government

1947 Marries Jo Bouillon; purchases Les Milandes in the Dordogne Valley

1949 Opens Les Milandes to the public

1951 Josephine Baker Day is held in Harlem on May 20; the Stork Club incident takes place on October 16

1952 Serves as a representative of Argentine dictator Juan Perón

1954 Adopts the first 2 of her 12 children

1961 Is named a Chevalier of the Legion of Honor by the French government

1963 Attends the March on Washington on August 28

1964 Suffers a heart attack in July and a second one in October

1969 Is evicted from Les Milandes; moves to Roquebrune near Monte Carlo, Monaco, with her children

1973 Appears at Carnegie Hall in New York City; suffers another heart attack and a stroke

1975 Opens in the revue *Josephine* at the Bobino Theater in Paris on April 8; dies of a cerebral hemorrhage on April 12

Archer-Shaw, Petrine. *Negrophilia: Avant-Garde Paris and Black Culture in the 1920s.* New York: Thames & Hudson, 2000.

Baker, Jean-Claude. *Josephine Baker: The Hungry Heart.* New York: Random House, 1993.

Baker, Josephine, and Jo Bouillon. *Josephine.* Translated from the French by Mariana Fitzpatrick. New York: Harper & Row, 1977.

Bechet, Sidney. *Treat It Gentle.* New York: Hill & Wang, 1960.

Bogle, Donald. *Brown Sugar: The History of America's Black Female Superstars.* New York: Continuum International Publishing Group, 2006.

Bricktop, with James Haskins. *Bricktop.* New York: Atheneum, 1983.

Colin, Paul. *Josephine Baker and La Revue Nègre: Paul Colin's Lithographs of Le Tumulte Noir in Paris, 1927.* New York: Harry N. Abrams Inc., 1998.

Flanner, Janet. *Paris Was Yesterday, 1925–1939.* New York: Viking Press, 1972.

Haney, Lynn. *Naked at the Feast.* New York: Dodd, Mead, 1981.

Klurfeld, Herman. *Winchell: His Life and Times.* New York: Praeger, 1976.

Long, Richard A. *The Black Tradition in American Dance.* New York: Rizzoli, 1989.

Papich, Stephen. *Remembering Josephine Baker.* Indianapolis, Ind.: Bobbs-Merrill, 1976.

Rose, Phyllis. *Jazz Cleopatra: Josephine Baker in Her Time.* New York: Doubleday, 1989.

Schroeder, Alan. *Ragtime Tumpie.* With paintings by Bernie Fuchs. Boston: Joy Street Books/Little, Brown, 1989.

Shack, William A. *Harlem in Montmartre: A Paris Jazz Story Between the Great Wars.* Berkeley, Calif.: University of California Press, 2001.

Stearns, Marshall, and Jean Stearns. *Jazz Dance: The Story of American Vernacular Dance.* New York: Macmillan, 1968.

Thorpe, Edward. *Black Dance.* New York: Overlook, 1990.

WEB SITES

FBI records showing investigation of Josephine Baker's purported Communist affiliations
(search for "Josephine Baker" under the "Alphabetical Listing" link)
http://foia.fbi.gov/room.htm

Josephine Baker (biographical information)
www.whyy.org/education/denycegraves/baker.html

Josephine Baker (with clips of her singing)
www.redhotjazz.com/josephinebaker.html

Josephine Baker: Image and Icon
http://sheldonconcerthall.org/baker.asp

News broadcast of Baker's citizen's arrest of a racist in Los Angeles
(then enter "Josephine Baker" into the search engine)
www.historychannel.com/broadband/home/index.jsp

The Official Site of Josephine Baker
http://www.cmgww.com/stars/baker/index.php

Alan Schroeder is an honors graduate of the University of California, Santa Cruz. His first book, *Ragtime Tumpie* (1989), was a fictionalized account of Josephine Baker's childhood in St. Louis. *Ragtime Tumpie* was selected by several magazines as one of the best children's books of 1989. It was also named a Notable Children's Book of 1989 by the American Library Association.

Heather Lehr Wagner is a writer and editor. She is the author of more than 30 books exploring social and political issues and focusing on the lives of prominent Americans. She has contributed to biographies of Harriet Tubman, Sojourner Truth, Thurgood Marshall, Malcolm X, Frederick Douglass, and Martin Luther King, Jr., in the BLACK AMERICANS OF ACHIEVEMENT, LEGACY EDITION series. She earned a B.A. in political science from Duke University and an M.A. in government from the College of William and Mary. She lives with her husband and family in Pennsylvania.